MW01487241

anger, fear, domination

introduction

This book advances three propositions: that what I call the dark passions—anger, hatred, humiliation, resentment, fear, and the drive for domination—fuel today's attacks on liberal democracy; that persuasive public speech is the main way demagogues mobilize these passions to pursue power; and that countering demagogues requires not only more responsive public policies but also a form of ameliorative rhetoric that defenders of liberal democracy have nearly forgotten. Although dark passions suffuse the rhetoric of autocrats who have already gained power, they are available for use by aspiring autocrats in liberal democracies as well. In unfavorable circumstances like the ones in which we now find ourselves, they endanger institutional restraints, the rule of law, civil rights and liberties, and democracy itself.

The authors of the U.S. Constitution were anything but blind to these passions—and to the threat they posed to the constitutional order. They hoped that the artful arrangement of countervailing institutions would form an impregnable barrier against demagogues with autocratic intentions. We are now testing the limits of this hope.

The defense of liberal democracy rests on a realistic understanding of political psychology, free from any illusion about the dominance of reason in public affairs. Today's proponents of liberal democracy should focus less on Rousseau and more on Hobbes, less on Walt Whitman and more on James Madison, less on John Dewey and more on St. Augustine. Democracy's defenders cannot defeat its enemies without understanding the enduring power of the passions to which they appeal—and how best to blunt this appeal. Of all the forces weakening liberal democracy today, its defenders' naïveté about human motivations may be the most dangerous.

Because human beings bring themselves in full to politics, those who wish to understand politics need a psychology as rich as the political life they seek to comprehend. The Greeks knew this; too often, we forget it or set it aside in search of a more tractable simplicity.[1] A dyadic psychology of reason and self-interest leaves too much out. So does a triadic psychology that focuses on ameliorative sentiments such as empathy, solidarity, and love.[2] Politics more often elicits harsher emotions, and when passions surge, even self-interest gives way. We can neither grasp nor conduct politics successfully unless we reckon fully with emotions like rage and the desire for revenge. If we hope to cabin their destructive power, we must put them at the center of our attention.[3]

To focus on dark passions is not to engage in psychological reductionism, which is both patronizing and misleading. Although the capacity for dark passions lurks within us all, their emergence is rarely random. Thinkers as diverse as Jon Elster, Martha Nussbaum, and Jan-Werner Müller have rightly insisted that passions have cognitive content. They represent reactions, often morally laden, to events. If we believe that others have treated us unfairly, our anger reflects this judgment. If we feel we are treated with contempt, our resentment expresses this judgment. If others resent us, it is always wise to ask what we may have done to evoke or even warrant this reaction. In politics as in families, passionate eruptions are usually a sign that some aspect of the status quo needs to change, including the attitudes and assumptions that guide our understanding.[4]

It is not my purpose to lurch from the extreme of optimistic liberal rationalism to its opposite. Reason can prevail in courts of law and in legislative deliberations, especially when they are conducted privately. And not all sentiments are dark. Hope can be inspiring, and so can appeals to justice, courage, compassion, and sacrifice for a collective good. If we care about a goal, we want to believe that it can be achieved, and great speakers—in sports, in politics, and in war—can infuse us with the confidence and determination to pursue it.

But too often, a rhetorical Gresham's law exerts itself, and the dark passions prevail. When things are going badly, we are tempted to seek someone to blame—a focus for an anger born of frustration—rather than believe that things can get better. The desire to punish others for our distress goes deep. We do not know whether public programs will improve our lot, but we feel that attacking our perceived enemies will give us a measure of satisfaction. When we turn the tables by gaining power over those who we think have wronged us, our instinct is to take revenge. Only rarely can great leaders like Nelson Mandela persuade us to choose the path of forgiveness and reconciliation. In normal times, with leaders who lack Mandela's greatness of soul, we have only one choice—to shore up the norms and institutions that safeguard free societies against autocracy while doing what we can to reduce the dark passions' destructive intensity. Even flawed leaders can rise to the occasion, and when they do, it is our civic duty to support them, however much partisanship and ideology may divide us from them.

Robert Frost famously defined a liberal as someone too broad-minded to take his own side in an argument. Although this is a caricature, it points to a real risk. But it is also risky to believe that all truth and virtue lie on one side of the divide and we have nothing to learn from those who oppose us. Even in times of deep division, honorable compromise is often possible, but only if we can listen with open minds to those whose views we mistrust. When the dark passions dominate public life, we must redouble our effort to find paths away from violence and toward politics—that is, to persuasion and other nonviolent means for making public decisions. But concerning the worst of our dark passions—hatred—politics fails. Hatred cannot be appeased; it can only be opposed—by force if it threatens to destroy what it loathes.

In free societies, homogeneity of sentiment and belief is not expected. Enabling us to live together peacefully is the first duty of responsible liberal democratic leaders. When we yearn for civic harmony, we expect too much from politics, but when we yield to unchecked strife, we expect too little. We must look to persuasive speech to bolster the institutions that protect us from tyranny and direct our politics toward whatever betterment is achievable.

I have divided this book into three sections. Part I addresses the complex relation between liberal democracy and the dark passions, focusing on liberal hopes that societies built on reason and self-interest would reduce the destructive passions' impact on political orders. Part II offers an anatomy of the dark passions, with chapters on anger, humiliation, and resentment; on fear and what we fear; and on the urge to dominate others. Part III illustrates how the misuse of speech can mobilize these passions—and how leaders can combine far-sighted policies with public-spirited rhetoric to tame them.

.

Part I

The Role of the Passions in Democratic Politics

I the multiple vulnerabilities of liberal democracy

The Core of Liberal Democracy

In the familiar term "liberal democracy," *liberal* is not the antithesis of *conservative* but rather of *total*. Liberal democracy is limited democracy, a form of government in which the power of democratic majorities is limited in multiple ways—by a protected zone of privacy, by individual rights, by constitutions—written and unwritten—and by a commitment to the rule of law. These restraints delimit not only the legitimate ends majorities may pursue, but also the legitimate means they may use to achieve them. In liberal democracies, the ends do not justify the means because the distinction between permitted and forbidden means serves the overall objective of protecting individuals and minorities against tyranny.

Some contemporary critics of liberal democracy confuse it with "neoliberalism," a market-based approach to economic policy that favors globalization, free trade in goods and services, unfettered movement of capital across national borders, and minimal regulation of domestic economic activities. As theory suggests and history confirms, liberal democracy as a political system is compatible with a wide range of economic arrangements but is not synonymous with any of them. The United Kingdom did not cease to be a liberal democracy when it adopted the socialist-tinged Beveridge Report after World War II—or when, a generation later, it enacted Margaret Thatcher's anti-socialist program. In practice, most liberal democracies have moved toward some version of a welfare state that collectively provides for human needs that the market does not meet for all citizens, and that uses regulatory power to rein in what the public regards as market excesses.

Despite its inadequacies, liberal democracy is the best form of government possible in our current circumstances. Over the past century, every effort to replace it with something different has led to something worse, and there is no reason to think the next century will be different. While there is space and need for searching debate about reforms of economic, social, and institutional arrangements, political responsibility in our time requires the improvement, not the replacement, of liberal democracy.

The Argument in Brief

The attack on liberal democracy is more pervasive today than at any time since the 1930s. Despite the gathering strength of its external enemies, this form of government is more likely to perish from within—from public dissatisfaction with its vulnerabilities, from demagogues' ability to mobilize popular passions against it, and most of all, from the myopia and naïveté of its defenders.

This mobilization of passions is to some extent inevitable. The defenders of liberal democracy are the true conservatives of our time, seeking to preserve what is good about the present as the best basis for future improvements. It is far easier to be passionate about abrupt and radical change, especially for those who have no experience—or historical knowledge—of the ills such change can produce. And antipathy offers satisfactions that more affirmative sentiments cannot match.

But there are deeper reasons for liberal democracy's vulnerability to the dark passions. While there are many ways of telling liberalism's creation story, the one that best fits the historical facts begins in the sixteenth and seventeenth centuries, when religious and secular writers mounted an attack against aristocratic pride and religious zeal, the passions they saw as most inimical to peace and social order. They offered self-interest guided by reason as the counterweight to destructive passions, and they advocated religious tolerance and commercial endeavor as the most effective ways of organizing societies that could contain and ultimately replace these passions.

By the end of the nineteenth century, many liberals had come to regard this form of social organization, often labelled "bourgeois," as an inevitable and irreversible result of scientific and moral progress. Military skirmishes would continue, of course, but dense commercial ties among nations had rendered great wars irrational, and therefore inconceivable.

The First World War destroyed this confidence, clearing space for philosophical challenges to liberal democracy and for revolutionary regimes that rejected both liberalism and majority rule as their organizing principles and rehabilitated religious zeal in the guise of secular ideology. The horrors of World War II reinforced doubts that rational self-interest could contain the dark side of human nature, giving rise to a generation of chastened liberals for whom fear was as fundamental as hope.[1]

As Europe rebuilt, economies and welfare states grew, international commerce flourished, colonialism shrank, liberal democracy spread, and the United States and the Soviet Union settled into an uneasy modus vivendi, the lessons learned between 1914 and 1945 gradually faded, and confidence became once again the dominant liberal sentiment. With the fall of the Berlin Wall in 1989 and the collapse of the Soviet Union two years later, liberal triumphalism surged, setting the stage for the latest round of disappointment. Neither Russia nor China democratized, the global spread of democracy reversed, religious zeal resurfaced, the cost of globalization became evident, nationalist passions intensified, and the spread of cultural liberalism generated a backlash. As internal divisions deepened within liberal democracies, long-muted passions reemerged, as did the kinds of leaders who knew how to use these passions for illiberal purposes. These developments blindsided liberals, who had come to regard the movement toward tolerance at home and internationalism abroad as irreversible.

Humbled once again, today's defenders of liberal democracy must set aside their illusions about human nature and history. The dark side of our nature is here to stay, and liberal democracy is a human creation that can buckle under pressure from the passions. Noble dreams have their place, but rigorous realism offers the best defense against the threats we now face.

That liberal democracy is under attack and on the defensive is no longer news. The wave that boosted it around the world peaked in 2006. Since then, some liberal democracies have declined qualitatively while others have morphed into nonliberal democratic forms of government.[2]

The friends of liberal democracy have awakened to the threat posed by autocratic states, of which Russia, China, and Iran are the most dangerous, and by leaders who practice what Hungarian president Viktor Orbán misleadingly terms "illiberal democracy"—an electoral system without safeguards for the civil rights of individuals and minorities or the civic rights of freedom of the press and of political opposition.[3]

Despite the gravity of these external challenges, liberal democracies are more likely to be undermined from within—by inherent vulnerabilities that cannot be eliminated, only managed, and by comforting illusions that the friends of liberal democracy must discard if they are to prevail.

The Inner Vulnerabilities of Liberal Democracy

As the post–World War II generation of liberal democratic leaders forged new, highly successful domestic and international institutions and policies throughout the West, the weaknesses of liberal democracy that dominated the two decades after World War I faded from view. But they did not disappear.

First, because liberal democracy restrains majorities, it slows the achievement of goals that majorities support. This generates frustration with institutional restraints, and an unacknowledged envy of authoritarian systems that can act quickly and decisively. China can build huge cities in the time that it takes the United States to review the environmental impact of small highway projects. Liberal democracy requires more patience than many possess.

Second, liberal democracy requires tolerance for minority views and ways of life to which many citizens are deeply opposed. It is natural to feel that if we consider certain views or ways of life to be odious, we should use public power to suppress them. In many such cases, liberal democracy requires us to restrain this impulse, a psychological burden that some will find unbearable.

This leads directly to the third inherent problem of liberal democracy—the distinction it requires us to make between civic identity and personal or group identity. For example, although we may consider certain religious views false and even dangerous, we must, for civic purposes, accept those who hold these views as our equals. They may freely express these views; they may organize to promote them; they may vote, and their votes are given the same weight as ours. The same goes for race, ethnicity, gender, and all the particularities that distinguish us from one another.

This requirement often goes against the grain of natural sentiments. We want the public sphere to reflect what we find most valuable about our private commitments. Liberal democracy prevents us from fully translating our personal identities into our public lives as citizens. This too is not always easy to bear. The quest for wholeness—for a political community, or even a world, that reflects our most important commitments—is a deep yearning to which illiberal leaders can always appeal.

Nor is the fourth inherent difficulty of liberal democracy—the necessity of compromise—easy to bear. If what I want is good and true, why should I agree that public decisions must incorporate competing views? James Madison gives us the answer: in circumstances of liberty, diversity of views is inevitable, and unless those who agree with us form a majority so large as to be irresistible, the alternative to compromise is inaction, which is often more damaging, or oppression, which always is.

Some always prefer purity to compromise, and sometimes they are right. The Israeli political philosopher Avishai Margalit has distinguished between tolerable compromises and "rotten" compromises—agreements so deeply flawed that no morally conscientious person should accept them.[4] But applying this distinction is not easy. For example, Margalit regards the compromise with slave states that made the U.S. Constitution possible as a rotten compromise; better, as the abolitionists argued, for the free states to have gone their own way. But Abraham Lincoln disagreed, and rightly so.

Some thinkers regard contemporary liberals' acceptance of diversity as weak-kneed. Rather than maintaining neutrality among different ways of life, liberals should endorse certain ways of life as superior and use democratic institutions to promote them. Samuel Moyn, for one, argues that liberals should place John Stuart Mill's belief that "the highest life for human beings is creative experimentation and originality" at the heart of their creed.[5] Mill insists that a life pursued according to one's own "plan of life" is superior to one lived in accordance with custom and tradition, which require only "ape-like" imitation.[6] The refusal of today's liberals to endorse this affirmative vision of what makes life valuable, Moyn claims, undermines liberalism's appeal.

Here's the problem: while many liberal democratic citizens agree with Mill, others do not. Some Americans believe that lives lived in accordance with tradition and the dictates of religion are superior to those that reject these sources of authority. If there is a Creator, then the "self-creation" Moyn endorses is of limited value. If American liberal democracy were to give official preference to the Mill/Moyn conception of good lives and use its institutional power to promote this conception, many citizens would conclude that their equal standing in American society had been called into question.

Moyn's proposal, the secular equivalent of establishing a state religion, would yield endless strife. The alternative—accepting and valuing diverse conceptions of good lives—is the only way that allows us to live together despite our differences. This does not mean that liberalism is comprehensively neutral. Liberals favor peace over war, plenty over penury, freedom over tyranny, and the rule of law over rule by decree. They embrace the moral equality of all human beings and the equal civic standing of all citizens. They believe that individuals enjoy a zone of immunity from state power. And they insist that consent, not coercion, is the basis of legitimate political authority.

Liberalism endorses a conception of social perfection—civic concord based on respect for others' right to live as they see fit—rather than individual perfection, and democratic institutions are used to safeguard civic space for the enactment of difference. Nothing in this conception prevents citizens from living Millian lives, but nothing requires them to do so.

This idea of social perfection as the freedom of equal citizens brings me to the final ensemble of liberal democracy's inherent challenges: the tangled relationship between liberty and equality, and the tendency of each to exceed its rightful bounds. As Tocqueville observed, the passion for equality can overwhelm the commitment to liberty; in the pursuit of ever-greater equality, core individual liberties can be abridged—or surrendered.

The converse is also true: in the pursuit of more expansive freedom, the legitimate concerns of equality can be ignored. Since Aristotle's time, the relationship between decent republican governance and a strong middle class has been well understood. But contemporary liberal democracies have not always attended to the impact of economic change on middle-class and working-class families, opening themselves to attacks from both the illiberal Right and the authoritarian Left.

The problem extends beyond potential imbalances between equality and liberty. Each, considered by itself, can lose its balance. Taken too far, equality can deny the existence—and legitimate claims—of excellence. Taken too far, the exercise of liberty shades over into what many see as license or outright moral anarchy. A liberal democracy faces the perennial challenge of keeping liberty and equality—its core commitments—in balance and within appropriate bounds.

Liberal Illusions

I turn now to the final category of threats liberal democracy faces—the unforced and avoidable errors of understanding that have weakened its defenders' ability to resist its adversaries. These illusions fall into three groups—myopia, parochialism, and naïveté.

Myopia. Today's defenders of liberal democracy often suffer from what might be termed myopic materialism: the belief—especially pervasive among elites—that economic issues are the real issues and that cultural issues are diversions, deliberately heightened by unscrupulous leaders to gain support for their anti-liberal agendas. This quasi-Marxist framework (economics is the base, everything else is the superstructure) denies the autonomy and power of cultural issues. Today's populists and autocrats know better. They advance their cause by battling their liberal adversaries on the terrain of culture, invoking traditional gender roles and moving such issues as homosexuality, same-sex marriage, and transgenderism to the front lines of the struggle. They oppose most immigration, not only on economic grounds but also because immigrants can challenge, and eventually change, long-established cultural traditions.

At the heart of culture is religion, whose persistent power liberals often underestimate. For example, as the most recent Turkish election campaign began, many observers believed that the country's economic downturn and runaway inflation would end President Erdoğan's two-decade grip on power. This view became even more dominant after Erdoğan's halting response to an earthquake that destroyed a generation of infrastructure development and ended or disrupted the lives of hundreds of thousands of Turkish citizens. The international community was stunned when Erdoğan led by 5 percentage points after the first round of balloting and then won reelection with 52 percent of the vote, about the same share as in the previous presidential election five years earlier.

To be sure, Erdoğan had done everything to tilt the playing field in his favor, leading many international observers to conclude that the election had been free but not fair. But this was nothing new. Rather, Erdoğan's religious rural and small-town base had kept him in power. Pious women were especially fervent in their support. Before Erdoğan, they explained, they could not get government jobs if they wore headscarves. Now they can. By ending the Kemalist tradition of strict secularism in public life, Erdoğan had made them full citizens for the first time, no longer forced to choose between religious observance and providing for their families. Until liberals—mostly clustered in large cities and national capitals—make the effort to understand the enduring influence of religion and traditional morality in the hinterlands, they will continue to be surprised by political events.

Parochialism. Many defenders of liberal democracy espouse some form of transnationalism, whether concrete ("citizens of Europe"), diffuse (the "international community"), or universal ("citizens of the world"). From this perspective, national boundaries and loyalties are forms of irrationality. We are all brothers and sisters under the skin, and the moral claims of sub-Saharan refugees are as important as those of our fellow citizens.

These views, however sincere, are not widely shared. Transnationalism is the parochialism of elites. Most people throughout the world value particular attachments—to local communities and to the nation, to friends and family and compatriots.

"Liberal nationalism" is neither oxymoronic nor obsolete, and good liberal democrats are not morally barred from giving extra weight to the interests and views of their fellow citizens. This does not mean that we can ignore the suffering of refugees, but the responses required of us may be limited—rightly—by our special attachments. Universal utilitarianism is a philosophical theory inapplicable to the real world of politics.

So is the view that all human beings want the same things. Yes, there is a universal aversion to the great evils of the human condition—poverty, famine, pestilence, and violence. And if the U.S. Declaration of Independence is correct, all human beings are morally equal and possess inalienable rights. It does not follow, however, that everyone wants to live in a liberal democracy. The need for security often trumps the desire for democracy; many individuals experience freedom as a burden, not an opportunity; and a sense of superiority, individual or collective, often drives out the awareness of moral equality. Ignoring these realities leads to expensive mistakes, such as believing that liberal democracy inevitably will emerge when tyrants are removed.

Naïveté. Of all the liberal illusions, naïveté about the course of human events and the possibilities of human nature is the most damaging.

In the nineteenth century, many liberals embraced the belief that the world was tending inexorably toward liberty, prosperity, and peace. By 1918, four years of bloody trench warfare had instructed the next generation of liberals on the limits of reason in human affairs. The rise of fascism reinforced the lesson, and the Holocaust convinced the post–World War II generation that destructive urges were inherent in our nature. Secularists found support for this proposition in Sigmund Freud's theory of the "death drive"; believers, in the writings of Reinhold Niebuhr, who famously called original sin "the only empirically verifiable doctrine of the Christian faith."[7]

As the horrors of two world wars gave way to rising prosperity and peace in Europe and between the great powers, the belief in progress returned. By 1962, John F. Kennedy could say that the problems liberal democracies faced were no longer ideological but technical and managerial—the selection and implementation of the best means to agreed-on ends—and that science, social as well as natural, could tell us which means were preferable.[8]

After the fall of the Berlin Wall and the collapse of the Soviet Union, many once again believed that history moves in only one direction: toward the permanent victory of liberal democracy over other forms of governance. American presidents of both political parties claimed that certain policies were on "the wrong side of history" or that practices could not persist because they belonged to the past.[9]

Sadly, history has no side, and regression to past horrors is always possible. The Balkan wars of the 1990s dented European confidence that mass brutality in the "heart of Europe" was unthinkable. Western leaders were shocked, but should not have been, when Vladimir Putin invaded Ukraine. In a post-invasion interview that offered a crystalline distillation of this illusion, former secretary of state Condoleezza Rice said, "I thought we had moved beyond . . . fighting for territory, thinking in ethnic terms, using resources to wage war," adding, "This wasn't supposed to happen. We thought the linearity of human progress should have left all of this behind"—as if history's magic wand would purge resentment and the urge to dominate from the human soul.[10]

Our commitment to liberal democracy must not be entangled with faith in the inevitability of progress. Change is inevitable, but it can be for the worse and often is. Progress is possible but not irreversible.

No doubt progress is real in some domains. Humans understand more about the natural world, and to some extent the social and political world, than we did centuries ago. These advances in human understanding have brought technological progress on many fronts, including medical innovations that have corrected physical dysfunction, diminished pain, and increased longevity. There has been material progress too; the share of humans living in abject poverty is much lower than it was just decades ago.

There is less evidence of moral progress. As China has shown, even broad-based economic gains and an expanding middle class do not guarantee movement toward civil liberties, let alone liberal democracy, and tentative gains in freedom of speech and thought can evaporate. Wars continue to rage on several continents, and innocent civilians continue to die. Governments continue to seize hostages and use them as instruments of state policy. Some governments reject democratization and mobilize ethnic majorities against disfavored minorities, and nations once committed to equal treatment of religious minorities shift toward theocracy. "Never again" is a commitment, not a guarantee, and it can give way in practice to "once again."

The possibility of regress is not an argument against aspirational politics, but it is a reminder that efforts to change the world based on confidence in progress can backfire. Past ills can recur, and pure intentions do not guarantee desirable results. Grasping these facts defines political responsibility. Critics of the status quo have a duty to offer more than vague hopes for a better world.

The mistaken faith in historical progress goes hand in hand with psychological naïveté. The defenders of liberal democracy tend to believe that some combination of reason and self-interest suffices to explain human behavior. This leaves out most of the sentiments that shape political life, including anger, hatred, humiliation, resentment, fear, and the lust for domination. Ordinary people often resent their treatment at the hands of elites, and entire countries can be driven by a sense of national humiliation—Germany after the Treaty of Versailles, China after what most Chinese call the century of humiliation from the 1840s to the 1940s, and Russia after the collapse of the Soviet Union. Viktor Orbán continues to inveigh against the Treaty of Trianon, the post–World War I agreement that stripped Hungary of more than half its territory and left millions of Hungarians as minorities in other countries. The desire to strike back often contradicts self-interest as conventionally understood, but this does not weaken the motivating power of revenge.

It is necessary, if almost embarrassing, to restate the obvious. An attraction to evil is part of human nature, and some humans succumb to it. Some people enjoy dominating others—subordinating them, humiliating them, gratifying lust, and inflicting unspeakable cruelties. The conflict between these perverse pleasures and liberal democracy's commitment to the moral equality of all human beings is self-evident.

Defects of our nature that fall short of absolute evil also pull against liberal democracy. There are those who glory in war and find no satisfaction in peace. There are those whose passion for imperial conquest overrides boundaries and national sovereignty. International laws and norms by themselves will not protect liberal democracies against these passions. To maintain peace, we must prepare for war. To resist aggression, we must be prepared to defend ourselves by force.

Recent events highlight the costs of forgetting these basic truths. After the Berlin Wall fell and the Soviet Union collapsed, Europe's leaders came to believe that core principles of the post–World War II order had become inviolable and that Kant's dream of perpetual peace was becoming a reality, at least for Europe. When Vladimir Putin invaded Ukraine and the West rallied to Kyiv's cause, it became apparent that European nations had allowed their capacity for self-defense to erode. Their armed forces had withered, and so had their ability to produce armaments that others could use. To resist Russian forces, Ukraine needs more than 1 million artillery shells each year, which Europe promised to provide, only to discover that its weakened defense industrial base could not do so.

The capacity for self-defense requires fighters as well as arms, and no conception of liberal democratic citizenship is complete unless it recognizes this reality. In times of war, doing what we want gives way to doing what we must, and there is no guarantee that there always will be enough volunteers to do our fighting for us. When I was young, "Make love, not war" was—understandably—a popular slogan, but it is often not a viable policy. At roughly the same time, John Lennon asked us to imagine a world without countries, a world in which human beings have no reasons to kill one another. Whatever the merits of this dream, it is not the world we live in, or will live in, unless human nature undergoes a fundamental transformation. Without those who are willing to die for liberal democracy, liberal democracy itself will die.[11]

In sum, those who wish to strengthen the ability of liberal democracies to resist illiberal and anti-democratic assaults must begin by shedding their illusions and embracing a rigorous realism about human nature and human history. Rational self-interest does not always drive human events, the passions matter, and evil is real. Economics isn't everything, or even the "base" of everything; culture and religion will not lose their independent power to shape understanding and motivate action. Nor does history guarantee the victory of liberal democracy over its adversaries. Nothing does, because it always remains possible to mobilize the dark side of our nature against efforts to build a better world.

2 liberalism and the dark passions

It may seem odd to regard Thomas Hobbes—often seen as an advocate of despotism—as a founder of modern liberalism. But the historian Noel Malcolm observes that Hobbes's theory contains "some of the most important building-blocks" of modern liberal political thought, including "the crucial role of consent; natural rights; egalitarianism; [and] the idea of the state as a device to protect people against oppressors." Hobbes also defended the rule of law and the concept of the state as a public realm rather than the property of any individual, family, or interest group. To be sure, he preferred monarchy to democracy. But he acknowledged that democracy was a form of government to which the people could legitimately consent—and that his preference for monarchy rested on prudential considerations whose validity was not self-evident.[1]

Hobbes's theory of politics rested on an understanding of human passions as potentially disruptive of the security most people crave. While he feared the passions, he hoped that one of them—fear—could be used to overcome the others. If we are rational about fear, he argued, we can escape from it.

Hobbes laid out this thesis in deservedly famous passages in his *Leviathan*. If there is no sovereign political authority to maintain order, he argued,

> there is no place for industry, because the fruit thereof is uncertain, and consequently no culture of the earth; no navigation, nor use of the commodities that may be imported by sea; no commodious building; no instruments of moving, and removing, such things as require much force; no knowledge of the face of the earth; no account of time; no arts, no letters, no society; and which is worst of all, continual fear, and danger of violent death; and the life of man, solitary, poor, nasty, brutish, and short.[2]

Especially notable in this list is his emphasis on the economic consequences of disorder—the disruption of production, harvests, trade, and construction—as well as of intellectual progress, social relations, and personal security. Hobbes's account of the evils of anarchy closely tracks the liberal (some would say "bourgeois") understanding of the purposes of political community.

So does his account of the path away from tyranny—the application of reason to the passions that "incline men to peace"—the fear of death, the desire for material prosperity, and the hope they can attain prosperity through work. Building on these passions, Hobbes argued, reason suggests "convenient articles of peace," including the agreement of individuals to surrender a portion of the liberty they enjoy in conditions of anarchy to a political authority—provided that all other parties to the agreement do the same. Civil liberty is the equal liberty of all members of the political community, liberty voluntarily diminished to attain human goods that cannot be secured by individual agents in the absence of a political guarantor. Establishing such a guarantor is self-interest rightly understood.

For Hobbes, then, hope rested on a foundation of fear. Political authority, the rational response to fear, creates an arena in which we can endeavor to fulfill our hopes. But history confirms Hobbes's belief that threats to political authority will never disappear, even when authority seems secure, because not everybody regards violent death as the worst evil. Some people are not satisfied with equal liberty. Because they think themselves superior to others, they crave honor, distinction, and power and are willing to upset the established order to get them, even at the risk of their lives. Religious zeal also can lead to civic disruption, especially when it offers zealots rewards in the afterlife. Political authority can suppress such people but never eliminate them. Passions incompatible with civil peace are not an eradicable disease but a permanent aspect of the human condition, and naïve optimists who forget this reality jeopardize the existence of the decent societies they take for granted.

Liberals who built on Hobbes's foundation maintained that his argument fell short in several key respects. First, he overestimated the scope of liberty that individuals were willing to surrender to achieve civil peace. For example, Hobbes argued that the sovereign should determine the beliefs—including religious beliefs—that would be compatible with public order. But exercising this authority turned out to provoke disorder, because many individuals saw liberty of conscience and belief as the core of the freedom they expected the sovereign to secure. John Locke's

Letter Concerning Toleration was an important contribution to the public debate that ultimately moved liberty of thought, speech, and religious practice to the center of the liberal creed.

Political thinkers since Aristotle had distinguished between monarchs who governed in the public interest and tyrants whose rule was guided by personal interests and beliefs. Hobbes would have none of this. Tyranny, he said, was merely monarchy "misliked," a subjective judgment, devoid of moral or political force, offered by disgruntled subjects. He feared anarchy so much that he downplayed the risks of tyranny and the need to protect the political community against the passions of the sovereign.

Later liberals could not follow him down this road. John Locke wrote that "freedom of men under government" means "not to be subject to the inconstant, uncertain, unknown, arbitrary will of another man."[3] The Federalist Papers are filled with references to tyranny and tyrants, and the bulk of the Declaration of Independence is devoted to evidence that George III had crossed the line from monarchy to tyranny. As James Madison famously formulated the problem in Federalist 51, "In framing a government which is to be administered by men over men, the great difficulty lies in this: you must first enable the government to control the governed; and in the next place oblige it to control itself." Although democratic thinkers would add a third task—enabling the people to control the government—Madison's thesis remains relevant.

Nor did later liberals agree with Hobbes that the parties to the social contract could not change the form of government they had created. Locke insisted that the logic of the contract implied a right of revolution, to be invoked when government ceased to promote the goods for which it had been established, and America's revolutionaries followed him in this respect. In short, political authority was neither total nor irrevocable, and this conception of limits to government came to define liberalism.

Another element of Hobbes's political thought received a divided response among later liberals. Some accepted his depiction of the dark side of human nature and designed political institutions that they hoped could withstand the destructive passions. Others, of a more optimistic bent, hoped that social progress would eventually reduce the intensity of these passions and their impact on politics.

Beginning in the eighteenth century, these hopes focused on the psychological effects of life in commercial societies. In *The Spirit of the Laws,* Montesquieu wrote that "it is almost a general rule that wherever the ways of man are gentle there is commerce; and wherever there is commerce, there the ways of men are gentle."[4] A decade later, Voltaire offered a witty portrait of commerce as the antidote to religious passions:

> Go into the London Stock Exchange—a more respectable place than many a court—and you will see representatives from all nations gathered together for the utility of men. Here Jew, Mohammedan and Christian deal with each other as though they were all of the same faith, and only apply the word infidel to people who go bankrupt. Here the Presbyterian trusts the Anabaptist and the Anglican accepts a promise from the Quaker. On leaving these peaceful and free assemblies some go to the Synagogue and others for a drink, this one goes to be baptized in a great bath in the name of Father, Son and Holy Ghost, that one has his son's foreskin cut and has some Hebrew words he doesn't understand mumbled over

the child, others go to their church and await the inspiration
of God with their hats on, and everybody is happy.[5]

A decade after this, Boswell quoted Dr. Johnson to the same effect: "There are few ways in which a man can be more innocently employed than in getting money."[6]

There is an argument for what may be called commercial optimism. Wars and other struggles for dominance are at best zero-sum, dividing participants into winners and losers. (I say "at best" because such struggles can leave everyone worse off.) But economic transactions can be positive-sum, leaving all parties better off, and economic growth can foster more generous attitudes toward less advantaged members of society.[7]

Evidence to support this long tradition of optimism about the pacifying effects of commerce is unfortunately thin. The pursuit of wealth can reflect motives other than material gain: the drive to found something that bears one's imprint or name; the desire to be admired; the competitive quest for status; and a passion for control that extends beyond the firm to society at large.[8] And as history shows, the pursuit of gain can lead to appalling mistreatment of others—exploitation, indifference to suffering, even knowing cruelty. There was nothing "gentle" about nineteenth-century capitalism, or the gold and diamond mines of colonial powers.

But commerce offered another basis for hope: even if the pursuit of gain could not eradicate destructive passions, it could overpower them. If self-interested political leaders could be shown that wars were economically irrational, perhaps they would refrain from starting them.

In 1911, a British pacifist named Norman Angell published *The Great Illusion,* which argued that during the previous century, economic interdependence among the leading industrial nations had grown so much as to make war among them self-defeating, and hence unreasonable. The book touched a nerve and was soon translated into fifteen languages and sold more than 2 million copies.

The Great Illusion did not quite say that because war had become irrational it had become impossible. But buoyed by the book's enthusiastic reception, Angell could not resist taking this step. He stated in 1913 that "the cessation of military conflict between powers like France and Germany, or Germany and England, or Russia and Germany . . . has come already. Armed Europe is at present engaged in spending most of its time and energy rehearsing a performance which all concerned know is never likely to come off." At last, "Peace on earth" was more than a prayer; concrete historical forces were now making it a reality.

Angell's thesis had its share of skeptics. Alfred Thayer Mahan, the United States' leading maritime strategist, countered that despite what economic calculation might suggest, "ambition, self-respect, resentment of injustice, sympathy with the oppressed, hatred of oppression" were among the many reasons, generous as well as self-regarding, why war would persist.

One might have thought that the horrors of the First World War would undermine Angell's credibility. Instead, *The Great Illusion* went through six more editions, and in 1933 (of all years), its author received the Nobel Peace Prize.[9]

Although the rise of fascism and communism led Angell to modify his views, the hopes he crystallized never disappeared. As late as

1936, with the memory of the First World War's horrors still fresh, John Maynard Keynes could write that "dangerous human proclivities can be canalized into comparatively harmless channels by the existence of opportunities for money-making and private wealth, which, if they cannot be satisfied in this way, may find their outlet in cruelty, the reckless pursuit of personal power and authority, and other forms of self-aggrandizement."[10] He seems to have forgotten that the century of relative peace and prosperity after the Congress of Vienna also witnessed a flowering of anti-bourgeois sentiments—in particular, dissatisfaction with (sometimes contempt for) commercial activities and the self-protective timidity of bourgeois life.[11]

Decades after Keynes, the rise of the European Union as a force for economic interdependence led continental statesmen to believe that European wars had been consigned to the dustbin of history—hence their shock when ethnic hatreds triggered genocidal war in the Balkans. Similarly, growing economic interdependence between the West and a rapidly modernizing China led many strategists to project a new era of peaceful relations, bolstered by China's liberalization and eventual democratization in response to its rising prosperity and expanding middle class. The collapse of these hopes has yielded a raft of challenges that policymakers now struggle to meet.[12]

In times of chaos and strife, human beings crave the tranquility of daily life, and many are satisfied when they get it. But those who are not satisfied tend to include not only the potential leaders of their societies but also individuals whose aspirations extend beyond material comfort. Accounts of politics that neglect this dimension of the human condition are bound to be descriptively and normatively inadequate. Realism demands more than a narrow focus on achieving a political order within which individuals can pursue their self-interest.

Discontent with bourgeois life has a long and surprising history. Discussing the defects of a society devoted to market transactions, Adam Smith remarked that commerce "sinks the courage of mankind and tends to extinguish martial spirit." If the national defense is consigned to a narrow class of professional warriors, he wrote, the people grow "effeminate." Worse, their minds are "contracted, and rendered incapable of elevation," and the "heroic spirit is almost lost."[13] We may wonder whether empirical sociology would vindicate these judgments, but their influence on centuries of thinkers and social elites is beyond question. When the First World War poet Rupert Brooke denounced the "sick hearts that honour could not move" and welcomed the outbreak of the war as "cleanness," he drew on the tradition that juxtaposes the martial virtues to the alleged small-mindedness of daily economic and social life.[14]

It is hard for today's liberals to take these considerations on board. The idea of honor, in their eyes, smacks of aristocracy, and their horror of war obscures the merits of the martial virtues. To the lovers of peace and security, dying for a cause—religion, country, or simple dignity—is almost incomprehensible. But it is an enduring fact of human existence that some people are willing to do so, even if most are not, and our understanding of politics must be capacious enough to embrace it.

The appeal to passions and emotions is not always a bad thing. Rhetoric that summons hope and directs righteous indignation toward reform can be a powerful engine of positive change. More often, however, the appeal is to the dark passions—anger, hatred, humiliation, resentment, fear, and the urge to dominate—and the consequences are usually destructive.

These sentiments abound in today's politics. Vladimir Putin bitterly resents what he sees as the West's aggression against Russia during his country's moment of weakness, and as his invasion of Ukraine demonstrates, he is determined to restore as much of the Soviet Union's sphere of influence—and past glory—as he can. Xi Jinping wants history to remember him as the man who eliminated the vestiges of China's "century of humiliation." Narendra Modi has organized—for political purposes—Hindu India's resentment against its Muslim and Christian minorities. In tribal societies such as Ethiopia, fear of the Other has been deployed to bloody effect.

The contemporary West is hardly exempt from this brand of politics. During the 2022 French presidential elections, party leaders seeking to displace incumbent president Emmanuel Macron vied with one another to mobilize fear of (mostly Muslim) immigrants. One of them, Eric Zemmour, himself an immigrant and a Jew, openly embraced the "Great Replacement" narrative of the extreme Right, a trope that has also spread to the United States. Many political scientists believe that resentment of immigrants was the decisive issue in both the Brexit vote and the 2016 U.S. presidential elections, and that the anger of partisans against other partisans is the main driver of politics today.

Although the central role of the dark passions in politics seems incontestable, it is contested nonetheless. In an influential recent book, *Liberalism Against Itself,* Samuel Moyn accuses the "Cold War liberals" of adopting an unduly pessimistic account of human nature after World War II, undercutting previous liberals' call for transformative social change to enlarge the realm of human freedom. Following a war-torn century, the Holocaust, and the rise of totalitarian threats to liberal democracy, Moyn charges, Cold War liberals placed fear of the collapse of free societies into tyranny at the center of their thought, and accounts of human motivation based on Augustine's original sin or Freud's death drive replaced sunnier Enlightenment-based depictions.

Moyn regards these shifts as an overreaction to the events that provoked them. I disagree. After Hitler's murderous hatred drove 6 million Jews to death camps and Stalin's drive for absolute domination doomed millions of Soviet citizens, after the bloodiest war in human history, the sunny optimism of the Edwardian age could not be maintained. Acting collectively at the direction of leaders bent on destruction, masses of human beings proved themselves capable of enormous evil, a reality that no responsible thinker or leader, then or now, can ignore.

But realism about the dark side of the human soul does not rule out an aspirational liberal politics, as Moyn suggests it must. Many politicians influenced by Cold War liberalism expanded the role of government, not only to fortify liberal democracy against its inherent weaknesses but also to enhance individuals' ability to enjoy the blessings of liberty. Although Lyndon Johnson was hardly naïve about human motivation, he announced his Great Society in terms that mirror Moyn's call for a more progressivist, perfectionist, ambitious liberalism:

The Great Society . . . demands an end to poverty and racial injustice, to which we are totally committed in our time. But that is just the beginning. The Great Society is a place where every child can find knowledge to enrich his mind and enlarge his talents. . . . But most of all, the Great Society is not a safe harbor, a resting place, a final objective, a finished work. It is a challenge constantly renewed, beckoning us toward a destiny where the meaning of our lives matches the marvelous products of our labor.[15]

This may be as close as any American leader ever has gotten to the liberalism of self-development and Millian "creative experimentation and originality" that Moyn extols as the alternative to the liberalism of fear he blames for the rise of conservatism. This should not surprise us: nearly all the Cold War liberals who most influenced American politics were supporters of the welfare state, not of limited government.[16]

This combination of psychological pessimism and policy optimism has deep historical roots. Johnson's blend of realism and aspiration is consistent with the long arc of the American liberal tradition. The Federalist Papers are suffused with a wintry realism about self-interest, turbulent passions, and demagogues' drive for tyrannical power, as well as grand hopes for the future of the American experiment. "It seems to have been reserved to the people of this country," Hamilton wrote in Federalist 1, to decide whether "societies of men are really capable or not of establishing good government from reflection and choice, or whether they are forever destined to depend for their political constitutions on accident and force." As secretary of the treasury, he developed and implemented bold plans for government's role in the economy. Caution about human motives did not lead him to minimize the uses of public power, just as there is no necessary connection, in our time, between Cold War liberals' motivational pessimism and market-centered neoliberalism.

A realistic understanding of the human capacity for evil as well as good offers the only secure basis for ambitious reforms. Without a foundation of Hobbesian order, the effort inspired by T. H. Green's idealist liberalism to construct a British welfare state stood no chance. Conversely, it was the civil disorder and decline of the 1970s that led to its partial dismantling. In times of economic decline and civil strife, Moyn's liberal *summum bonum*— the achievement and exercise of individuals' ability to act creatively in the world—stands no chance.

The conclusions Cold War liberals drew from the disasters of the twentieth century precluded progressivist hopes for the steady improvement of the human condition, let alone the perfectibility of human beings. Unpredictable events and the vagaries of governance could expand or contract human freedom and self-realization. Progress was possible; so was regress. Just as there was no "new Soviet man," there can be no new liberal man. We are free to pursue aspirational politics, but with no guarantee that its achievements will be permanent.

Acknowledging the dark passions need not promote government retrenchment. On the contrary: understanding how they function in our lives helps define the conditions for a liberal politics that is ambitious but aware of democracy's inherent fragility.

Part II

An Anatomy of Dark Passions

3 anger, humiliation, and resentment

The sentiments that illuminate politics are as likely to reflect conflict as consensus, antipathy as affection. Antipathy may even be the dominant political sentiment. It unites individuals into communities of the like-minded and pits these groups against each other. Anger, far more than enthusiasm, mobilizes people to act, and shared antipathy is often the only force holding a group together.[1] When the object of antipathy disappears, the group splinters. Dictators always use antipathy to mobilize support and mute criticism. Democratic leaders, even those with positive agendas, often do so as well. In a speech capping his 1936 reelection campaign, Franklin D. Roosevelt declared of his enemies—business and financial monopolists, speculators, and reckless bankers, among others—"Never before in all our history have these forces been so united against one candidate as they stand today. They are united in their hate for me—and I welcome their hatred."[2] So did the crowd, which roared its approval.

Anger and Hatred Compared

I begin with the fundamental difference between anger and hatred. Anger is directed to agency, hatred to identity. We feel anger because of what someone has done, hatred because of who someone is. Offenders can seek to make amends for what they have done, but how can they make amends for what they are? Anti-Semitism is not anger toward Jews (although it often represents itself as that), but hatred of Jews, regardless of what they do or have done. The Iron Crosses German Jews earned during World War I availed them nothing under Nazi rule. If anti-Semitism had been directed at the religion of Judaism, European Jews could have saved themselves by converting. They could not, because their destroyers regarded being Jewish as an indelible identity rather than a choice.

The difference between anger and hatred plays out in human experience. With time, anger usually cools; hatred often persists indefinitely. Anger seeks to impose pain or punishment on its object, while hatred seeks the destruction of the Other. Anger seeks rectification for the wrongs the perpetrator has committed; for hatred there can be no rectification. Anger can be appeased; hatred can only be opposed. Anger can sometimes be abated by political means; the only remedy for hatred is forceful opposition. Hatred expresses itself in the raping and maiming of the enemy, and sometimes in genocide. Hatred motivated Hamas's rampage in southern Israel, the slaughter of the Tutsis in Rwanda, and of course, the Holocaust. Hitler's Germany has been rightly described as the only regime ever that had no clear principle other than "murderous hatred of the Jews."[3]

The Sources of Anger

The sources of anger are many. Most primal is the frustration of expectation or desire. We see this in the anger of infants who have not yet developed moral consciousness or a sense of self. But adults who seek to impose their will on events often experience something similar. Herodotus tells the story of Xerxes, faced with stormy waters that delayed his invasion of Greece, venting his rage by whipping the Hellespont.[4] The mature response to the impeding of one's will by inanimate objects is frustration, not anger; so too for unplanned collective events such as stock market crashes. In extreme cases, the anger-induced attribution of will to such forces can shade into paranoia.

The most common cause of anger is injury inflicted on you or a third party, deliberately or through inattention. The harm can take many forms—physical, material, social. Some people are angry about immigration, not because immigrants commit crimes or consume tax dollars, but because they change the character of communities. We can be angry about prospective as well as current injuries. Many people were angry about President Obama's Affordable Care Act long before it was signed into law, not because it cost money or restricted freedom, but because of fears that it would someday do so. Harm-based anger reflects our interpretation of intentions and circumstances, not just the injury itself. If another driver swerves out of his lane and hits your car, anger is the natural response, even if he was not ramming you for sport. The discovery that he was texting while driving is not likely to abate your ire. On the other hand, learning that he acted to avoid hitting a child who had dashed into the road should transform anger into another sentiment altogether. (If it does not, you are angry about something else.) Although we typically feel anger when someone has harmed us, we may also experience it as righteous indignation when we observe harms to innocent others, especially when the wrongdoers go unpunished.

A third occasion of anger is damaged pride. The classic example is Achilles sulking wrathfully in his tent after Agamemnon has taken Briseis from him. Achilles tells his mother, the goddess Athena, that Agamemnon "has done me dishonor." The injury is secondary; what rankles is the insult.

Honor is prominent in aristocratic societies, and so too, therefore, is sensitivity to dishonor. But insult and the anger it breeds manifest themselves in egalitarian circumstances as well. Dignity is honor democratized. Actions that breach dignity evoke rage, not only from the powerful and well-born but from the lowly and oppressed. On December 17, a young Tunisian man, Tarek al-Tayeb Mohamed Bouazizi, set himself on fire after suffering public humiliation, the details of which are disputed. But it is not disputed that he was harassed and extorted by government officials as he sought to support his family by selling produce from a wheelbarrow in the streets of his hometown, Sidi Bouzid. A female official seized his weighing scale, and the local authorities refused to return it. Powerless to strike back against the government to regain his livelihood and dignity, Bouazizi doused himself with gasoline and immolated himself. Instead of attacking his oppressors, he expressed his thwarted rage by destroying himself. Bouazizi became a symbol of an entire generation's humiliation at the hands of its government, triggering massive street protests, the ousting of Tunisia's longtime leader, and eventually the Arab Spring.

No doubt the spread of egalitarian sentiments has raised the aspirations of oppressed groups and their awareness of deprivation. But the desire for dignity—the recognition of one's standing as a human being—is more than a social construction. This desire helps explain the attractiveness of the ideas that ratify its legitimacy and give it force as a constitutive principle of social order. To be human is to be liable, as Mohamed Bouazizi was, to the injury of humiliation. The tension between subjection to the will of others—even legitimate authority—and the desire for dignity is a permanent feature of the human condition.

Humiliation, Rage, and Political Conflict

Of all the variants of anger, the most powerful, and often the most dangerous, is anger born of humiliation. Wherever we look we see individuals, groups, entire nations seething over affronts to pride, dignity, or self-respect. Several philosophers have looked at the statics of humiliation—what it is.[5] I am more interested in its dynamics—what it does. Still, it is useful to begin by describing its central features.

The word *humiliation* is derived from *humus,* the Latin for earth or dirt. This points to a core dimension of humiliation: bringing someone down from a height. Toppling statues of deposed dictators symbolizes this process; so does making people prostrate themselves before you or kiss your shoes. To humiliate is to degrade, to reduce someone to a lower position in rank or estimation. The French Army's treatment of Alfred Dreyfus offers a vivid example:

> Each regiment of the Paris garrison had sent a unit to represent it. . . . A small door was thrown open. From it stepped a giant sergeant of the Republican Guard. He led four soldiers with drawn swords in whose midst walked Captain Dreyfus. They walked up to General Darras, who sat waiting for them on horseback. The general drew his sword . . . : "Alfred Dreyfus, you are unworthy of carrying arms. We herewith degrade you in the name of the people of France." Dreyfus . . . lifted up his head. "Soldiers," he shouted, "An innocent is dishonored. Long live France." The giant sergeant rushed at Dreyfus. He tore the epaulets from the captain's shoulders and then tore the red stripes . . . from [his] trousers. Finally he took the captain's sword and broke it in two.[6]

As Frederick Schick points out, Dreyfus was not ashamed; he knew he had done nothing wrong. Still, he was humiliated, and a closer analysis of this episode explains why. Dreyfus was deprived of agency and strength; he was rendered helpless and weak, deprived of control over his fate. He was disempowered. Worse, his disempowerment was forced on his attention.[7]

Dreyfus's humiliation was very public. It was, in fact, the most publicly visible event in France at the time, and its visibility endured for years. Still, spectators are not essential. B can humiliate A even if no one else is there. B can experience humiliation because of how he behaved in A's presence, even if A did nothing to rub it in, even if A is unaware of B's assessment. Without abusing the term, B may believe he degraded himself. Humiliation requires only two parties, one of whom may be the agent's internalized spectator. When there are only two, however, the humiliated party must believe that his behavior was in some respect unworthy; otherwise, there is no humiliation. Dreyfus was brought low not in his self-estimation, but in the esteem of others. The public witnessing made it a humiliation, but Dreyfus did not experience the inner sentiment we call shame because he knew that he had done nothing wrong.

Although bringing someone down in rank or office is a classic instance of humiliation, it is not a necessary condition. Ordinary people may be, and often are, subjected to degrading treatment that qualifies as humiliation. Humiliation, say Jennifer Goldman and Peter Coleman, occurs in relationships of unequal power in which the humiliator has control over the victim.[8] U.S. treatment of prisoners at Abu Ghraib is an example; there are many others. Nazis sometimes ordered Jews to get down on their hands and knees and clean streets with toothbrushes. In an SS-run concentration camp, the guards ordered Jewish prisoners to take fallen autumn leaves between their teeth and move them one by one to the edge of the courtyard. Non-Jewish prisoners were commanded to watch and shout epithets (many courageously refused and turned their backs).[9] Evelin Lindner describes the use of public rape as a strategy of humiliation, made even worse by the authorities' refusal to take it seriously.[10]

As everyone who has survived high school knows, selective exclusion is a common strategy of humiliation. By depriving some individuals of the rights and opportunities that others enjoy, the power holders send the message that those they exclude are of lesser worth. Segregation almost always embodies such a message.

That is why separate is hardly ever equal, unless the dominant group takes separation to its limit by granting subordinate groups something approaching full autonomy.

Humiliated individuals and groups are always deprived of something. It may be a thing they have never possessed or enjoyed but believe they should, a goal blocked by their humiliator. In other cases, they once possessed or enjoyed what they desire, but the humiliator has wrested it from them, and they want it back. The line between these two kinds of humiliation can be indistinct: not infrequently, an oppressed group will create the myth of a glorious past, a high station it yearns to regain. In other cases, the deprivation is demonstrable: the decline of a once-great empire, the loss of territory, the transition from dominance to insignificance. The desire to regain what has been lost is one of the most potent motives in human affairs.

Defining Humiliation

So much for the description of humiliation; I turn next to its definition. Avishai Margalit, the best-known contemporary philosopher to address this topic, defines humiliation as "any sort of behavior or condition that constitutes a sound reason for a person to consider his or her self-respect injured." Otherwise put, humiliation is "injury to human dignity."[11] While these definitions link humiliation to familiar terms in moral discourse, the meaning of these terms is contested. It is conceptually possible to distinguish between pride and self-respect: the former, one may say, represents an overreaching sense of self; the latter a correct assessment of our standing as human beings. According to Spinoza, "Pride . . . is joy born of the fact that a man thinks more highly of himself than is just."[12] In this spirit (though against the letter of Spinoza), one might say that self-abasement is thinking less highly of oneself than is just, out of the self-hatred that can stem from the internalized prejudices of others, while self-respect is an accurate self-assessment gained through the exercise of reason and a sense of proportion.

But this move elides the central question: what does an accurate appraisal yield? From a familiar Christian perspective, unflinching introspection reveals us all as sinners. "Use every man after his desert," Hamlet muses, "and who shall 'scape whipping?"[13] We may want to become better, but we cannot improve through our own efforts alone. Without the aid of a divinity whose power and goodness infinitely exceed our own, we would remain mired in sin. Understanding our sinfulness and dependence on a higher power is true humility. An accurate self-appraisal means that self-respect and humility are one.

While the Christian account of human beings is egalitarian, it is unabashedly negative. We are equal because we are weak, fallible, divided against ourselves. Though equally egalitarian, the modern understanding of the self as the bearer of dignity, inherently worthy of respect, is much more affirmative. We are all capable of self-reflection and change through choice. This conception of the self might be described as the secularized version of the biblical proposition that we are made in the image of God, and hence capable of creativity, generosity, and wisdom.

Note that this is a normative definition in two senses. First, it does not regard inner sentiments as dispositive. One may have sound reasons for feeling humiliated but not actually feel that way; alternatively, one may feel that way without a good reason. If you are a member of a caste that has been systematically oppressed for generations, you may not have the internal experience of humiliation because you cannot imagine an alternative to the treatment you endure. (You may even have internalized your oppressors' justification for it.) Conversely, if you are a father within a tribal system of "honor codes," your daughter's refusal to marry the man you have selected for her may induce a sense of humiliation even though, judged from outside that culture, you lack a sound reason.

This brings us to the second sense in which Margalit's definition of humiliation is normative: he assigns the experience a thoroughly negative evaluation. If one accepts the classic Christian view that pride is the worst sin and humility the greatest virtue, then the normative status of humiliation becomes more complex. Because humiliation (like all suffering) counters pride and fosters humility, as Christian theology teaches, it is not an unmixed evil, even if the humiliator is driven entirely by base motives. This may be why Christian martyrs often thanked their humiliators for bringing them closer to God through suffering.[14]

With this, we have moved from a static definition of humiliation to the Christian account of its dynamics. But historical experience makes it hard to defend that account. On balance, Nietzsche's depiction of *ressentiment* seems closer to the mark. When the strong humiliate the weak, the oppressed typically experience anger, which their circumstances require them to repress. But the anger remains and fosters the desire for revenge.

Despite this difference, all these accounts of humiliation share a common premise: the opinions and actions of others affect our sentiments and our self-assessment. Humiliation, Doron Shultziner and Itai Rabinovici suggest, means "treating people or displaying attitudes in a way that conveys the message that they have lower, or no, social worth."[15] This message, they suggest, generally has an effect. Human beings seek recognition from others. Being deprived of the recognition they crave is experienced as an injury to self-worth—that is, as humiliation.[16]

Stoicism challenges this assumption by claiming that self-respect is bestowed by the self on the self and cannot be externally provided, withheld, or impaired. This sharp division between inner and outer runs counter to much ordinary experience. Nietzsche regarded it as psychologically impossible. Shakespeare underscored the conflict between the Stoic Brutus's professions of invulnerability and his actual sentiments. Still, some individuals have approached the Stoic ideal. Frederick Douglass, while traveling through Pennsylvania, was once forced to sit in a train's baggage car. When a white passenger expressed regret that Douglass had been "degraded" in this manner, the abolitionist leader and former slave replied, "They cannot degrade Frederick Douglass. The soul that is in me no man can degrade. I am not the one that is being degraded on account of this treatment, but [rather] those who are inflicting it upon me."[17] Throughout his life, Douglass burned with anger over the injustice of slavery and second-class citizenship. But because he was armored against humiliation, his righteous anger never shaded over into the desire for revenge. Other political actors—Nelson Mandela, Václav Havel—whom powerful oppressors tried to humiliate seemingly endured the experience without giving way, at least in public, even to anger.

These extraordinary individuals represent one of the three responses to socially inflicted humiliation—the ability to rise above it. This response is the hardest, and it would be unwise to rest either theory or practice on the presumption that this inner self-sufficiency is widely shared. For most people at most times, a sense of self-worth and dignity reflects, in part, society's favorable judgment and respectful treatment, the denial or withdrawal of which is acutely painful. Some who experience this pain respond by turning their humiliation inward to depression and self-destruction.[18] Others turn it outward to expressions of moral outrage that call on humiliators to mend their ways, or to rage that enacts the desire for revenge.

The most systematic research finds, for example, that mass shootings are "acts of personal desperation performed by humiliated individuals, almost all of whom are men. They finally lose control after they have brooded for a long time over supposed personal insults or injuries for which they feel unable to get satisfaction any other way."[19]

Humiliation and cold-blooded murder are linked on the political as well as personal level. The connection between humiliation and terrorism is well established. A leading expert, Jessica Stern, describes the internal dynamics of terrorism in terms nearly identical to those used to describe mass killers: "It is the pernicious effect of repeated, small humiliations that add up to a feeling of nearly unbearable despair and frustration, and a willingness on the part of some to do anything—even commit atrocities—in the belief that attacking the oppressor will restore their sense of dignity."[20] A good example is found in the statement of a masked terrorist on a videotape showing the beheading of American captive Nicholas Berg. Referring to photos showing the mistreatment of Iraqi prisoners at Abu Ghraib, he says that "the shameful photos are evil humiliation for Muslim men and women in the Abu Ghraib prison" and asks, "Where is the sense of honor, where is the rage? Where is the anger for God's religion? Where is the sense of veneration of Muslims, and where is the sense of vengeance for the honor of Muslim men and women in the Crusaders' prisons?"[21]

The Political Dimensions of Humiliation

Social theorists have long wrestled with the movement from individual to group psychology. There is no need to posit a perfect isomorphism, let alone a mysterious group soul. For my purposes, the connection is straightforward: when individuals think of themselves as members of a collectivity, they experience what befalls the collectivity as their individual fate. This capacity for sympathetic identification is ubiquitous among humans, from the elation sports fans experience when their team wins to the dejection and fear citizens feel when their country's army is defeated.

Some defeats are honorable, others not. In losing 1-0 to Germany in the 2014 World Cup, the U.S. team was thought to have acquitted itself well. By contrast, the citizens of Brazil experienced their team's 7-1 defeat as a national humiliation, and the sense of collective disgrace was palpable. The 1940 collapse of the French Army in the face of the German onslaught was a profound shock to the nation's self-respect, and much of General de Gaulle's wartime strategy was directed toward regaining French dignity. The Arabs' stunningly swift defeat at the hands of the Israelis during the Six-Day War of 1967 was a collective humiliation that their leaders felt impelled to overcome.

As in the individual case, there are two variants of collective humiliation. In the first, oppressive power prevents a group from asserting its claim to equal standing. The oppressed group is deprived of the ability to determine its own fate, a status it experiences as a denial of dignity. The group may never have enjoyed independence. Still, the denial of self-determination is a deeply felt affront that demands collective self-assertion. This dynamic is at the heart of anti-colonial movements, all the more so when colonial powers justify their rule through the language of racial or civilizational superiority.

In the second form of collective humiliation, the group has been deprived of something it once possessed and regards as its own by right, a loss comparable to physical mutilation. The loss often occurs in the wake of a military defeat that is felt to be dishonorable, producing seething resentment and a desire for collective revenge, of which territorial irredentism is a classic manifestation—France after 1870, Germany after 1918, and Pakistan after 1948. Germany's humiliation at Versailles was the emotional trump card that Adolf Hitler played effectively for nearly two decades. It fueled his rise to power and sustained him throughout the 1930s. His economic and diplomatic successes helped restore national pride and marginalized his critics. Without this fund of exploitable humiliation, the Nazi triumph would have been unimaginable.

Although Germany's experience of Versailles was as fresh as an open wound, the memory of national humiliation can be very long—indeed, all but indelible. Serbia's defeat by the Ottomans at Kosovo Polje in 1389, which paved the way for centuries of Turkish rule, drives Serbian nationalism to this day and helps explain why the Serbs bitterly opposed the Kosovar independence movement in the 1990s.

The desire to regain what has been lost and to punish the group or state that took it cannot be reduced to a means/ends calculus—economic, demographic, or military. It is a matter of injured self-regard, of dignity and honor. The reason/interest dyad explains the affairs of nations no better than it explains the motives of individuals. As Robert Harkavy observes, "Were revenge seen as a major component of international relations, foreign policy models based on assumptions of realism, rational choice or rationality would be weakened."[22]

Sometimes the loss is larger and less specific, such as when a great empire or civilization declines to relative insignificance. Yet not all such losses lead to enduring resentment. There is no evidence of a burning desire to re-create the Austro-Hungarian Empire. During World War II, Winston Churchill famously declared, "I have not become the King's First Minister in order to preside over the liquidation of the British Empire."[23] Once the war ended, however, this is exactly what happened, a momentous shift in Britain's global standing to which most Britons responded with nostalgia and regret rather than anger.

The contrast with Russia could not be sharper. Vladimir Putin's speech to the Duma of March 18, 2014, passionately articulated a litany of grievances against Western policies since the collapse of the Soviet Empire.[24] He said that his predecessors had "humbly accepted" the inclusion of Crimea as part of Ukraine in 1994 because at the time, post-Soviet Russia was "incapable of defending its interests." Nevertheless, he declared, "the people could not reconcile themselves to this outrageous historical injustice." The remainder of the speech extended this conclusion more widely, as one would expect of a leader who regards the collapse of the Soviet Union as the greatest historical tragedy of the twentieth century. In the immediate aftermath of the speech, an overwhelming majority of Russians endorsed Putin's stance, as they did after his invasion of Ukraine in February 2022.

China offers a subtler but equally pertinent example. According to the late China scholar William Callahan, "The master narrative of modern Chinese history is the discourse of the century of national humiliation."[25] In this account, aggressive foreigners exploited corrupt rulers to undermine Chinese sovereignty and occupy much of the country. The decades following the First Opium War (1839–42) saw a long sequence of failed rebellions, military defeats, and political decline. Though lifelong adversaries vying for command of modern China, Mao Zedong and Chiang Kai-shek agreed on the need for a program of national salvation to overcome China's humiliation and restore its greatness. As Callahan observes, national salvation entailed more than a domestic agenda: "notions of 'the rightful place of China on the world stage' continually inform Chinese foreign policy in both elite and popular discussion."[26] The drive to overcome humiliation encourages a definition of China's "sacred territory" as extending to the outer perimeter of the Qing dynasty and reinforces claims to contested islands well outside what international law recognizes as China's territorial waters.

To the outside world, China's "fall and rise" story appears extraordinary. From the inside, the restoration of what China has lost is far from complete. Americans see the U.S. Navy's growing presence in the South China Sea as the minimum needed to keep faith with their friends in the region and to honor American treaty commitments. From the Chinese perspective, the U.S. fleet is an aggressive foreign presence, an unwelcome reminder of an era in which foreign powers dismembered and dishonored their country.

The Muslim world presents what may be today's most potent narrative of collective humiliation.[27] After dominating much of the Mediterranean region for centuries, Islam entered a long cultural and military decline. The Christian reconquest of Iberia was a heavy blow, and the Crusades became an enduring metaphor for Western incursion into regions Muslims regarded as the heart of their world. The collapse of the Ottoman caliphate and its colonial partition after World War I meant a demeaning loss of agency throughout the Sunni world. British domination of the Iranian oil industry had a similar effect on Shi'a Islam. The covert Anglo-American operation that helped overthrow populist prime minister Mohammad Mosaddeq in 1953 set the stage for a generation of struggle against the shah, who was seen as the tool of Western interests.[28]

The restoration of dignity has become a major theme of contemporary Muslim politics, especially after a series of humiliating defeats at the hands of the Israelis beginning in 1948. The Six-Day War was the Waterloo of the secular Arab nationalism that Egyptian leader Gamal Abdel Nasser represented. Muslims asked what in their culture and political systems could pave the way for such a defeat, and many blamed the adoption of Western ideologies and institutions. After 1967, the Islamist political alternative became increasingly attractive, as did stricter versions of Sunni and Shi'a Islam. For many Muslims, the stunning victory of the Khomeini forces in the 1979 Iranian revolution, followed swiftly by the storming of the U.S. embassy and the taking of hostages, represented long-overdue steps toward restoring their independence and dignity.

Humiliation and the Limits of Self-Interest

I do not mean to defend, let alone ennoble, political conduct driven by humiliation. My point is that the sources of humiliation are rooted in the human condition. To be sure, social arrangements shape how individuals and groups experience others' behavior. Acts that would be humiliating in hierarchical societies may not be in egalitarian settings, and vice versa. Hobbes hoped that the recognition of equal vulnerability might purge society of the disruptive force of hair-trigger aristocratic pride. But the belief in equal dignity carries its own disruptive potential. Populists can be just as sensitive to slights, real or imagined, as elites. When average citizens believe that those with wealth or education are "looking down" on them, their response can be ferocious.[29]

The politics of humiliation is even more dangerous in relations between nations. Peoples driven by a sense of loss are apt to exaggerate past glory. The drive to regain lost standing often overreaches, imposing pain on others and affronting their dignity in turn. Policies motivated by a desire for revenge can easily turn brutal and end by denying the adversary's humanity. Only when the spirit of vengeance cools can interests be negotiated.

In the quest to regain honor or dignity, individuals often make choices that appear irrational, even self-destructive. So do peoples. Egypt launched the 1973 Yom Kippur War against Israel not so much to reconquer the Sinai as to regain the pride it had lost six years earlier. The war ended with the Israelis crossing the Suez Canal and encircling Egypt's Third Army. Still, in the eyes of most Egyptians, the war achieved its primary objective. Their soldiers' bravery and bold tactics had earned respect from friend and foe alike. Despite its ultimate failure, the attack enabled the Egyptians to deal with Israel as equals, not supplicants. If 1973 had not muted the humiliation of 1967, Anwar Sadat could not have flown to Tel Aviv in 1977 and made peace with Menachem Begin in 1979.

We cannot understand these events without paying attention to humiliation and its consequences. We need a moral psychology rich enough to do justice to these phenomena. This is hardly a new thought. Plato's tripartite account of the soul gave independent status to *thumos*—spirited self-assertion—as distinct from the satisfaction of appetites and basic needs. Aristotle's *Rhetoric* offers a systematic account of the passions in a moral and political context. Rousseau distinguished between *amour propre* (the self-esteem that comes from the approval of others) and *amour de soi* (the concern for oneself that exists even in isolation). Hegel emphasized a desire for recognition powerful enough to overcome the instinct for self-preservation. And Hobbes, the apostle of political order based on self-preservation, knew well that two forces—prickly pride and religious fervor—could disrupt that order. When these forces combine, as they do in narratives of Muslim humiliation, they become explosive. Hobbes would not have been surprised.

The point is not that a politics of honor or dignity is nobler than a politics of interests, or that risking one's life is more worthy than risking one's capital. It is rather that the desire for standing, whether equal or superior, differs qualitatively from the desire for comfort and security. No account of politics can be adequate if it fails to recognize this difference. Humiliation may explain conduct but does not suffice to justify it. At most, humiliation invites an inquiry into the events that evoke it, and into the possibility that those events represent an injustice that should be rectified. Even if there was an injustice, rectification need not be whatever the humiliated actor demands, since those demands are often punitive and disproportionate. In this regard, humiliation is on all fours with self-interest, whose demands often lack justification.

Resentment

Resentment often leads to anger but is distinguishable from it. Resentment shapes much (many would say too much) of today's politics, especially but not exclusively on the Right. It is volatile, and dangerous if ignored.

The etymology of the word offers a guide to the experience. *Resentment* is literally an emotion that is "felt again"—repeatedly. Anger can be transitory; it can flare and burn out. Resentment smolders. Resentful people review—sometimes obsessively—the wrongs that gave rise to their feeling. They brood over them even as, like Shakespeare's Iago, they conceal what they feel.

Some acts that provoke resentment are unavoidable and appropriate. Many of us resent being told what to do, even if we know we should do it. Many of us resent being rebuked, even when we know the criticism is justified. We bridle at the stance of moral authority our critics adopt, even when they are right. We experience all this as a diminution of our sense of self, and of our equal standing.

My focus, however, is on the kind of resentment that we can hope to avoid or at least mitigate—resentment as a distinctive response to the perception of being treated unjustly, unfairly, or disrespectfully. Unlike the anger to which it can give rise, this resentment remains bottled up. Resentful individuals often don't give voice to their feeling because they feel helpless or because they fear retaliation. Fear can stem from a sense that speaking out would lead to social disapproval, economic loss, or even physical attack. The sense of helplessness comes from the disproportion between your own power and that of the institutions or individuals who are wronging you.

Resentment is often hard to spot unless you are looking for it and get close enough to see it. This explains why observers are so often surprised when it bursts forth as anger or rage.

What brings on this eruption? First, those who are already seething experience a triggering event, such as the killing of George Floyd, and just can't take it any longer. Second, individuals who think they are alone gradually encounter like-minded others, a process the internet accelerates, and through this mutual discovery overcome their sense of helplessness. Third, leaders emerge who give voice and legitimacy to suppressed sentiments, helping their new legions of supporters feel powerful enough to act.

Some resentful people want a remedy for the injustice they have experienced. But others—typically those who experience disrespect—want more than redress; they want revenge.

As Iago brooded over the promotion Othello had denied him, he did not seek a reversal of this decision. He wanted to "own" Othello—and to destroy him. He succeeded in both, and in so doing, destroyed himself.

Resentment is one of the most powerful forces in human life. Unleashing it is like splitting the atom; it creates enormous energy that can lead to honest discussions and long-delayed redress of grievances. But resentment can also undermine personal relationships and political regimes. Because its destructive potential is so great, it cannot be ignored, as today's politics of resentment in the United States and throughout much of Europe so vividly underscores.

4 fear and its family

Americans of a certain age vividly remember how their lives felt in the 1990s. The alliance that the United States led for decades had brought down the Soviet Union without firing a shot, and projections that Germany and Japan would seize global economic leadership from us seemed increasingly far-fetched. Liberal democracy was on the march, as was the market-based economic model. Globalization was our friend, and the wind was in our sails. The fruits of economic growth were broadly shared, and we felt secure in the world. The "end of history" turned out to be a holiday from history, but it felt good while it lasted.

All this seems very long ago. In just a few years, the sense of security was swept away, replaced by pervasive fear. The 9/11 attacks destroyed the illusion that we lived in a world without dangerous enemies, and the global financial crisis undermined confidence in market mechanisms and the experts who claimed they could manage them. Increased competition from China combined with technological change to destroy millions of man-ufacturing jobs and undercut rural economies, and a grindingly slow recovery from the Great Recession fueled fear that large por-tions of the population would be left out of the new economy, with no chance to recover what they had lost. With the pandem-ic's enforced dislocations and deprivations, fear gave way to re-sentment, and then to anger. Rapid demographic and cultural change added fuel to this fire.

We were left with two Americas divided by dueling fears. One America fears being deprived of its liberty to live as it always has, in stable communities where its traditions and religious beliefs can find full expression. The other America, welcoming the dem-ographical and cultural changes of recent decades, fears that efforts to resist these changes have mutated into an attack on lib-eral democracy.

Both sides have a point. Both feel under attack. And as Thucy-dides observed, fear of loss can lead to war, including—as our own history teaches—civil war.

Fearing Fear

The descent from fear into chaos and violence is not inevitable. In his first inaugural address, FDR famously declared his "firm be-lief that the only thing we have to fear is fear itself—nameless, unreasoning, unjustified terror which paralyzes needed efforts to convert retreat into advance." This proposition has a distin-guished lineage. Michel de Montaigne acknowledged, "The thing in the world I am most afraid of is fear." Two centuries later,

Henry David Thoreau echoed Montaigne: "Nothing is to be feared as much as fear." Eleanor Roosevelt believed that her husband took the thought from Thoreau, while historians note that it was prominent in the popular culture of FDR's youth.[1]

On its face, the idea contradicted common sense. With the unemployment rate standing at 25 percent as FDR assumed office, many Americans who still had jobs feared losing them. Joblessness broke up marriages, destroyed people's self-respect, and turned thousands into homeless vagabonds. The Depression had shuttered the banking system, and people lost their life savings or feared losing them. Many thought the constitutional order would be undermined and that America's democracy would go the way of Europe's. None of these fears was unfounded or exaggerated.

Nonetheless, FDR's declaration does make sense, *if* we give due weight to the words that follow the dash. He feared not all fear but a specific kind of fear—terror—that deprives us of the ability to act against the sources of our fear by diminishing our sense of agency and driving out our power to reflect on our circumstances. He understood that the response to fear is not limited to "fight or flight"; *freezing* is a frequently observed alternative (hence the proverbial "deer in the headlights").

This is not a new thought. America's Montaigne, Ralph Waldo Emerson, asserted that "fear defeats more people than any other one thing in the world."[2] Near the end of *Democracy in America,* Alexis de Tocqueville makes explicit the distinction that gives sense to FDR's words: "Let us, then, look forward to the future with that salutary fear which makes men keep watch and ward for freedom, and not with that flabby, idle terror which makes men's hearts sink and enervates them."[3]

FDR made this idea his own by casting it in military terms— retreat and advance. We are meant to think of terrified, disorganized soldiers fleeing the front lines. Literature is replete with leaders who step forward to rally their troops, halt their retreat, and prepare them to take the offensive. This process is not logical but psychological; it fights terror with hope—and with an element of shame as well. Cowardice is sometimes seen as rational, but never as honorable.

For FDR, this idea was deeply personal. Note the "paralyzes": the newly inaugurated president could not have used this word without thinking of his own struggle. After polio made him unable to walk, he could easily have withdrawn from public life and surrendered to his new condition. Instead, he struggled against his infirmity until the end of his life, and he never lost hope that the therapeutic waters of Warm Springs would restore at least some of what the disease had taken from him. Hope is not sufficient to overcome fear, but it is a necessary condition. Leaders can master seemingly overwhelming obstacles, but only if they can infuse others with hope.

Franklin Roosevelt's presidency ended as it began. In the last words he wrote, prepared for a radio address that a fatal cerebral hemorrhage left undelivered, he declared that "the only limit to our realization of tomorrow will be our doubt of today." And he concluded, characteristically, "Let us move forward with strong and active faith."[4]

Faith—the religious note was not accidental. The biblical dream of abolishing fear lay at the heart of this eminently practical man's agenda. In his "Four Freedoms" speech to Congress, delivered nearly a year before the United States entered World War II, FDR called for "freedom from fear, which, translated into world terms, means a world-wide reduction of armaments to such a point and in such a thorough fashion that no nation will be in a position to commit an act of physical aggression against any neighbor—anywhere in the world."

Twenty-five hundred years earlier, the prophet Micah imagined a world in which "they shall sit every man under his vine and under his fig tree, and none shall make them afraid."[5] FDR gave this vision an immediacy that the prophet had not dared. "That is no vision of a distant millennium," he insisted. "It is a definite basis for a kind of world attainable in our own time and generation."[6]

FDR's conviction had enduring consequences. Seven months after the Four Freedoms speech, and four months before Pearl Harbor, he and British prime minister Winston Churchill issued a joint declaration of postwar aims later dubbed the Atlantic Charter, which came to serve as the basis for the United Nations. "After the final destruction of the Nazi tyranny," the two leaders declared, they "hope to see established a peace which will afford to all nations the means of dwelling in safety within their own boundaries, and which will afford assurance that all the men in all lands may live out their lives in freedom from fear and want."[7]

The prophet's time horizon proved more realistic than the president's. Humanity seems destined to live with a measure of fear indefinitely. The practical challenge is not to abolish it but rather to abate it, and to harness what we cannot eliminate to the achievement of such security as a world riven by conflicts will permit.

Understanding Fear

FDR rightly implied a distinction between productive and counter-productive fear. There is, as well, a difference between reasonable and unreasonable fear. To see how this distinction works, let us repair to the foundational discussion of the matter: Aristotle's *Rhetoric.*

Fear, Aristotle tells us, is a "certain pain and perturbation arising from an imagining of [i.e., conceiving of] an impending ill that is destructive or painful."[8] The concluding words of this definition point to the principal categories of fear. One category of fear is the fear of loss—the anticipation that something we value will be taken from us. The other category is fear of harm, such as pain, that worsens our life even though nothing we ordinarily characterize as loss has occurred. It would be intelligible but odd to speak of "the fear of loss of the absence of pain." The harm is direct and unmediated.

Our sentiments can shift harms from one category to the other. If we once lived pain-free but now experience chronic pain, we can view our current pain as the loss of the more desirable prior condition. On the other hand, when the pain is present, we no longer experience it as fearful because it is no longer "impending" but actual. A homely example: when we are in the dentist's chair, we fear that the treatment will be painful. But once the drilling starts, we no longer fear pain; either we experience it or we don't.

And during a pause in the drilling, we often fear pain when it begins again, even if we did not experience it the first time.

Living without fear is an unreasonable hope because it is reasonable to fear the great evils of the human condition and because, as Aristotle says, some sources of fear are "beyond human endurance."[9] Only exceptional human beings can withstand the threat of torture.

Fear, then, is inevitable, because the sources of reasonable fear are perennial and there are limits to what human beings can bear with equanimity. But we can exercise a measure of control by cultivating the virtue of courage. The courageous person resists unavoidable fears as well as anyone can. More generally, Aristotle says, the courageous person "endures or fears the right things and for the right purpose and in the right manner and at the right time."[10] An excess of fear is cowardice; a deficiency of fear is insensitivity to circumstances—or indifference to the significant possibility of death or great harm.

The adjective *impending* marks another point at which fear can go wrong. "People do not fear things that are very far off," Aristotle observes. "All know that they will die, but because it is not close at hand, they give it no thought."[11] This is true, with a qualification. There are two senses of "fear." When great ills are immediate or highly possible, they evoke a distinctive psychological and physiological reaction, an inner sensation that affects our normal processes of reflecting and acting. But it is also possible to fear, in a cooler, more reflective manner, ills that are likely at some point in the future but not right now. The drafters of the Constitution feared tyranny as the worst political evil and did everything they could to prevent it, at the cost of other political goods, such as the ability to act quickly in nonemergency circumstances.

Fear has a cognitive component. For example, we can misjudge what is or is not impending. American officials had a hard time believing that Kabul would fall quickly, and so did many Afghans. This misjudgment may have cost some officials their jobs; it certainly cost some Afghans their lives. They should have been fearful but were not. Conversely, some people may act precipitately in the misguided belief that something far off is imminent. Climate change is real, but we should not imagine that the Greenland ice cap is about to fall into the sea. Knowing that we have time to prevent, or prepare for, a distant ill can lead to more effective responses than emergency policies typically produce.

Many other cognitive distortions affect our fears. We may imagine that something is very likely, even though its real probability is low, and squander resources in an unnecessary effort to prevent it. On the other hand, we may regard an occurrence as impossible because it is unimaginable. The Jews who remained in Germany after passage of the Nuremberg Laws could not believe that non-Jewish Germans would reject them as compatriots. Many German Jews had served their country with distinction during World War I, and they believed their Iron Crosses would protect them from persecution. Because their imagination was limited, they did not fear enough, and they paid for this misjudgment with their lives.

Aristotle's definition of fear reveals another point where its cognitive dimension can go wrong. We may be right that an event is impending but may misjudge it as an ill. People may fear going to the dentist because they expect the experience to be painful. We can agree with them, arguendo, that pain is bad while insisting that with modern anesthetics, they will not experience it in the dentist's chair. The same holds for vaccinations, which contemporary ultra-thin needles make virtually painless.

Experience or the lack of it can shape what we fear. Because a toddler who has never encountered hot stoves may touch one with no expectation of harm, parents spend a great deal of time trying to teach their children what is dangerous and what is not. People who have never sailed may not correctly interpret gathering clouds as a sign of a coming storm. Experience is a great instructor, but it is safer to learn about some ills indirectly.

Deliberate distortions may induce otherwise reasonable people to fear what should not be feared, or the reverse. There is no evidence that COVID-19 vaccines suppress fertility or alter our DNA, but reckless statements to this effect induced many individuals to avoid vaccinations that might have saved them from hospitalization and premature death. Mass gatherings can be super-spreader events, but people flocked to them as though this possibility did not exist.

Most people, and most politicians, believe that hope and fear are opposites and that hope is an antidote to fear. Aristotle dissents: when people feel fear, he contends, "some hope of salvation must endure concerning the matter over which they anxiously contend. . . . For fear renders people apt to deliberate, yet no one deliberates about hopeless things."[12] Yet there is a kind of fear—terror—that makes deliberation and action flowing from it all but impossible.

In the main, however, experience supports Aristotle's position. Fearful people do not want to be told there is nothing to be done about the source of their fear. They flock to leaders who validate both their fear and their hope, who reassure them that although the situation is grave, there is a way forward. This is why demagogues who play on people's fears present themselves as the cure. A Russian dissident of the Stalin era, Nadezhda Mandelstam, lucidly explained this complex intertwining: "Fear is a gleam of hope, the will to live, self-assertion. . . . Fear and hope are bound up with each other. Losing hope, we lose fear as well."[13]

When Alexander Pope wrote that "hope springs eternal," he could not know that Auschwitz and the gulag would confute him. But he was mostly right. Most of the time, individuals have a basis for restoring their lives, and political leaders have a foundation for saving their country. The task of politics in dark times is to transform hope into confidence.

Confidence, says Aristotle, is hope accompanied by the belief that "the things that bring salvation are nearby and that the frightening things either do not exist or are far-off."[14] The confidence that confident leaders exude can be contagious, and these leaders can enhance the effect of their personal example with reasons that make sense.

It is easy to focus on the infectious confidence with which Franklin Roosevelt delivered his first inaugural address and overlook its sustained argument for confidence. Fear distorts our judgment, FDR implied, because it makes the possible appear impossible. Look at our strengths, he urged his countrymen and -women: "Our distress comes from no failure of substance. We are stricken by no plague of locusts. Compared with the perils which our forefathers conquered because they believed and were not afraid, we have still much to be thankful for. Nature still offers her bounty and human efforts have multiplied it. Plenty is at our doorstep, but a generous use of it languishes in the very sight of the supply." Our democracy and our society are healthy, he assured his listeners, and our Constitution is flexible enough to deal with troubles the Founders could not have imagined. Our difficulties "concern, thank God, only material things." They were caused by the actions of short-sighted and greedy men. And because "the money changers have fled from their high seats in the temple of our civilization [we] may now restore that temple to the ancient truths." Roosevelt proceeded to sketch a program of action designed not only to convey a clear sense of direction but to persuade the country that confidence in a better future rested on a credible foundation.

Although confidence is bolstered by argument, it is an emotional state, not a rational proposition. Understanding this, FDR drew on martial sentiments to inspire confidence while invoking the martial virtues of courage and devotion to a cause. The challenge of the Great Depression represented the moral equivalent of war. "If we are to go forward," he declared, "we must move as a trained and loyal army willing to sacrifice for the good of a common discipline." And he would be its general: "I assume unhesitatingly the leadership of this great army of our people dedicated to a disciplined attack upon our common problems."

FDR understood, finally, that confidence is built on trust, and citizens trust leaders who share their values. For this reason, I suspect, the opening paragraphs of the first inaugural are suffused with references to the Hebrew and Christian Bibles, which served—then more than now—as America's common culture. The newly installed president audaciously quoted Proverbs— "Where there is no vision, the people perish"—presenting himself as democracy's prophet in a moment of national peril. The prophets warned and chastised, of course, but they never separated themselves from the people, and even in the darkest days, they always offered hope. Lest anyone miss the point, he ended his address by beseeching God to protect the people and guide his presidency.

Fear's Family

As FDR implied, there are states of mind and emotion akin to but distinguishable from fear. Terror is "unreasoning." It loses all sense of proportion about the threat, and sometimes about its source. It is fear without fear's cognitive dimension. The brain's executive function, which can weigh the choice between fight and flight, is overwhelmed. Even when it does not freeze us in place, it can yield to the undeliberated impulse to flee even if standing our ground would increase the chances of survival and success. Recall the horrible sight of people jumping to their certain death from the upper floors of the burning World Trade Center. An experienced firefighter would have explored every chance, however remote, of escaping through the flames. Perhaps the jumpers did, and decided that instant death on the pavement below was preferable to the agony of burning to death. But the more likely explanation is that they panicked, as nearly everyone without relevant training would have done.

At the other side of fear's family is worry or concern—fear without the immediacy. A financial official may express concern that a policy will lead to an unacceptable rise in inflation; a parent worries that a child in the military may be sent to the front lines. The threat, although clear, is only prospective, yet it is nonetheless present.

Individuals experience the future in different ways. For some, the prospect of distant ills has no impact on their conduct; for others, the future is vividly *present,* in both senses of the word. (Differences in imaginative capacities are probably at work here.) Many young adults are more concerned about climate change than their parents and grandparents are, in part because, unlike the older generation, they are likely to be alive in a world transformed by severe weather and rising seas. There is another dimension to the difference: for young people, experiencing current weather events narrows the gap between the present and the future, transforming concern into fear.

Assessments of probability also affect the gap between concern and fear. Many older adults worry that they will be afflicted with Alzheimer's disease or some other significant cognitive impairment, but adults with a family history of age-related mental decline are more likely to live in fear. An extreme example is Huntington's chorea, a neuro-degenerative disease caused by an inherited defect in a single gene. Because each of us inherits two copies of nearly every gene, each child of a parent with Huntington's has a 50 percent chance of developing the disease. With the odds this high, it would be difficult for at-risk young adults not to experience fear as a constant companion.

Some states of mind can be described as fear minus its object or trigger. Some people experience "free-floating" anxiety—a diffuse, chronic uneasiness and apprehension not directed toward any specific situation or object. Dread—fear without a specific object—is structurally similar to anxiety but far more intense. Recall the shower scene in Hitchcock's *Psycho*. Everyone senses that something horrible is about to happen to Janet Leigh, but no one knows what it will be. This nameless fear—dread—is more terrifying than any threat we can identify.

Some sentiments in fear's family reflect cognitive distortions. Systematically overestimating the probability that you will experience an adverse health event can make you live in a defensive crouch. Hypochondriacs are figures of fun in literature, but the harm they inflict on themselves is deadly serious. Other forms of mental disease—paranoia, for example—lead individuals to imagine nonexistent threats. The distinction between paranoia and justified fear rests on the distinction between what is real and what is not, a line that is hard to draw in times—such as our own—when a shared understanding of facts and how to ascertain them breaks down.

What We Fear

The capacity to feel fear is innate, and it is reasonable because we are vulnerable beings. Still, culture shapes the focus and intensity of our fears. Warrior cultures regard the inability to master fear as shameful; care cultures believe that individuals should be allowed to express their fears and should be protected against situations that trigger them.

Some cultures inflate our perception of vulnerability and encourage a sense of fragility rather than resilience. Other cultures go to the opposite extreme by fostering recklessness while downplaying obvious risks. The point of equipoise—a sober evaluation of the dangers we are exposed to—is hard to locate and even harder to maintain. It is difficult to assess the long-term consequences of current trends, and tempting to focus excessively on the remote possibility of major harms while overlooking threats that are much more probable. Some regard the "precautionary principle" that shapes European social policy as an example of this excess. If we discourage children from climbing trees, there will be fewer broken arms, but less of the confidence that only reasonable risk-taking can foster. "Safe spaces" may insulate us from our fragility at the cost of not learning how to stand up for ourselves and to distinguish minor annoyances from genuinely hostile environments.

Despite these cultural differences, some fears are inherent in the human condition. At the risk of belaboring the obvious, it is worth inventorying them.

Most people fear death—especially violent or premature death—except those whose firm faith in the afterlife allows them to accept with equanimity the prospect of their earthly demise. We cease to fear death only when we are ready to die, a state of acceptance reached by some elderly individuals and some experiencing unrelenting, untreatable suffering, physical or mental.

We fear pain—so much that the prospect of pain often exceeds the actuality.

We fear the great evils of the human condition—plague, famine, poverty, natural disaster, economic depression, and civil war.

We fear oppression, whether from foreign or domestic sources, and we fear the loss of liberty, even if we don't all define liberty the same way. But it cannot be an accident that incarceration—the loss of physical liberty—is a near-universal mode of punishment.

Speaking of which: we fear punishment because it deprives us of what we care about—life, liberty, property, regular communion with family, colleagues, and friends. Some religious believers fear punishments meted out by a just God, while others are comforted by the prospect of rewards in an eternal afterlife. But the complexities of religious belief are endless. Researchers hypothesized that Buddhist monks trained to meditate on the illusory nature of the self would fear death less than those without this training. They found the reverse: the sense of self is hard-wired, and thinking about death makes its prospect more fearful, not less.[15]

As we age, we fear the loss of physical and—even more—mental capacities. I have yet to meet anyone my age who does not regard with horror the loss of memory that defines our selfhood. The children of aging parents fear this too, because no longer being recognized by one's parent is enormously painful.

Parents fear losing their children, whether through death, mental illness, or the children's entrance into cults that persuade or force them to renounce their parents.

We fear the loss of intimate ties—the love of our family, the affection of our friends.

We fear, as well, the loss of civic and social ties. Most children of parents who brought them into the United States illegally as minors have grown up knowing no other country. Deportation would remove them from the culture that shaped them, and thrust them into an alien environment. Cancellation often turns alleged offenders into social pariahs, which is why so many people will silence themselves or confess to imaginary errors to avoid it.

We fear dishonor; more broadly, we fear acting in ways that forfeit the regard of our peers. Many soldiers fear being labeled cowards more than they fear injury or death on the battlefield. Firefighters rush into burning buildings, whatever the risk, rather than disgrace themselves by hanging back. Fear of disgrace deters most scientists from distorting the results of their experiments, and most authors from plagiarism.

We fear failure, not only because it deprives us of the prize we sought but also because it threatens to lower us in our own esteem and the esteem of others. Generals fear defeat on the battlefield, politicians at the polls. Businesspeople fear the reverses that can lead to dismissal or bankruptcy. Failure can be instructive, but only those with a pathological desire to undermine themselves will seek it.

We fear embarrassment, which is why so many of us resist revealing our mistakes—and why, as the Washington adage goes, the cover-up is often worse than the crime. For the same reason, we fear new forms of surveillance that can reveal our intimate secrets. Privacy protects us from fear—if we can rely on it.

Otherwise, the potential loss of privacy becomes one more source of fear.

We fear the loss of our physical homes, havens of comfort and memory, and also of the moral and cultural environment that shapes us and in which we feel most at home. Threats to "our way of life" unleash fears that can disfigure society and politics. As C. Wright Mills once observed, "When people cherish some set of values and do not feel any threat to them, they experience *well-being,* [but] when they cherish values but *do* feel them to be threatened, they experience a crisis. . . . And if all their values seem involved they feel the total threat of panic."[16]

When a faction in a community fears that another is determined to undermine its way of life, civil tensions can turn violent. Threats to cherished political institutions can trigger the same spiral of descent.

Many fear the unfamiliar. Evolution may have implanted a visceral need to distinguish between "us" and "them," a default setting that protects us against some dangers but exacerbates others. Resisting our instinctive mistrust of the "stranger" helps diverse societies work better, while giving way to this mistrust sparks efforts to resist and even reverse increasing diversity.

Some fear the future because they believe it will be worse than the past for themselves or their children. Rising percentages of Americans fear that their children will face diminished economic opportunities; others fear what they regard as a steadily degrading moral environment. About half of all Americans think we were a better country in the 1950s than we are today, and they foresee no end to what they regard as our moral decline.

Others do not fear the future and welcome change, either because they believe the arc of history bends toward the improvement of the human condition or because they regard change as the precondition for new experiences and possibilities. If continuity is safe and predictable, some of us will opt for change as the best antidote to boredom. Some young men welcomed the outbreak of World War I as a break from the monotonous safety of bourgeois life. Those with above-average tolerance for risk often endure setbacks, even disaster, but they can also change their societies and the world in valuable ways.

Still, uncertainty breeds fear when it fosters a sense that the pilot is flying blind, and accelerating change can breed fear when it fosters a sense that nobody is even in the cockpit.

Judging Fear

It is easy, but too simple, to view fear in purely negative terms. Fear is often an unpleasant experience, but if we could not feel it, we would lack an essential safeguard against danger. It alerts us to the possibility of harm and moves us to avoid or counter it. Fear would have no rationale *only* if we were invulnerable and immortal. In traditional theology, we have reason to fear God, but God has no reason to fear us.

In an extended critique of fear, Martha Nussbaum concedes that "fear of danger, when it is proportional and healthy, prompts evasive strategies that can make safety and health more likely."[17] As we learned during the pandemic, the unwarranted absence of fear can make things worse, for reckless individuals and for society.

Nussbaum asserts that fear is "intensely narcissistic. It drives out all thought of others." This is not always true. "Often," she acknowledges, "we do fear for our children and other loved ones." Then she squares the circle: "That just means that the self has become bigger."[18] By this reasoning, fear is narcissistic by definition: anybody or anything on whose behalf we fear is part of our extended self.

This move saves the theory but not the phenomena; it distorts the experiences we are trying to explain. Human beings have a capacity to care about individuals other than themselves. The fear we experience for others' safety and well-being is an expression of this care. Not feeling fear for others to whom we are connected would signal culpable insensitivity.

Fear driven by care takes political as well as personal form. We can fear for the future of our country, as many Americans do today. In response to increasing evidence of climate change, many people express fear for the future of the planet.

These fears can go too far, of course. Parents' excessive fear can stifle their children's development toward independence and maturity, leaving them risk-averse and unable to fend for themselves. In these circumstances, Nussbaum's charge of narcissism has force: parents claim to be protecting their children, but they are really protecting themselves from their own nightmare of loss. Excessive concern about one's country or the planet can reflect psychic mechanisms that are focused inward toward the individual rather than outward toward the world.

Some see fear as salutary—as an intense experience and a source of focus. Winston Churchill once remarked, "*Nothing* in life is so *exhilarating* as to be shot at without result" as intense fear gives way to equally intense relief.[19]

Others see fear as a cure for the decadence of daily life. Peace and prosperity—the classic goals of liberal society—degrade the soul, goes the argument; bourgeois life is morally small. Sentiments of this sort have animated intellectuals from the poet Rupert Brooke, who welcomed the outbreak of World War I, to the commentator David Brooks, who thought the 9/11 terror attack would wash away the Seinfeldian self-absorption of the 1990s.

The encounter with fear provides the occasion for as much courage as the human condition permits. Churchill claims that "courage is rightly esteemed the first of human qualities . . . because it is the quality which guarantees all others." Hannah Arendt echoes this thought: "Courage liberates men from their worry about life for the freedom of the world."[20]

Experience supports these judgments. Courage demonstrates, and makes real, care and concern for other individuals and for the community. If we are not willing to risk something on behalf of what we value, our professed care and concern are hollow declarations.

This truth does not settle the question of when we are required to give the recipients of our care and concern what Lincoln called our "last full measure of devotion." But John Stuart Mill poses the central issue: "A man who has nothing which he is willing to fight for, nothing that he cares about more than he does about his personal safety, is a miserable creature who has no chance of being free, unless made and kept so by the exertions of better men than himself."[21] As history attests, peoples unwilling to risk their lives to secure their freedom eventually lose it.

Courage may be an intrinsic good, as many moral philosophers have argued, but it is undeniably instrumental to the attainment and preservation of other goods that human beings regard as valuable for their own sake. We celebrate the first responders who rushed into the burning Twin Towers on 9/11. Their willingness to risk their lives for others excited spontaneous admiration, independent of its consequences for those in danger, most of whom could not be saved. At the same time, their action saved some who otherwise would have perished, a consequence we value in less exceptional circumstances as well.

Not everyone agrees that courage is fear's antonym. In place of courage, Nussbaum offers a triad of antidotes—faith, hope, and love. In effect, the classical virtue corresponding to a remedy for fear disappears, replaced by the Christian virtues. This is how she can devote an entire book to fear without once mentioning courage.

To be sure, we often make enormous sacrifices for those we love. But unless we love strangers as much as our family and friends, which few do, love will not move firefighters to risk their lives in burning buildings. Only devotion to duty, bolstered by courage, can do this.

The Politics of Fear

For centuries, a hallmark of what we now call the liberal tradition has been its determination to guard against the greatest political evils of the human condition—violent death and tyrannical oppression. Safeguards against these ills are foundational, and they take priority over institutions and practices designed to produce political goods such as justice.

Thomas Hobbes, who was born prematurely when his mother heard of the coming invasion of the Spanish Armada, once wrote that "my mother gave birth to twins: myself and fear."[22] Although fear of violent death—the *fons et origo* of bourgeois life—was at the heart of his approach to politics, he understood that not everyone put this fear first. Aristocrats risked death in the pursuit of glory, and fervent religious believers, certain of their reward in the afterlife, were willing to endure death to defend their faith. Those who prefer dying honorably to living dishonorably, Hobbes argued, are a threat to peaceful political order. He believed they needed to be inculcated with a fear of violent death in order to counteract commitments that threatened the order of society. They had to be persuaded that death is the *summum malum,* and courage had to be devalued relative to the peaceful virtues. Peace, Hobbes taught, was the precondition for the practices that produce material prosperity, the other great goal of liberal societies.

After the optimistic progressivism of the nineteenth century, the political disasters of the twentieth reminded the world of human beings' capacity for evil and strengthened the case for a politics that would defend against it. Utopian dreams were the problem, not the solution; we should focus on the *summum malum,* not the *summum bonum,* and adhere to the political equivalent of the Hippocratic oath. Judith Shklar argued for a "liberalism of fear," and Hans Jonas said we should "give the prophecy of doom priority over the prophecy of bliss."[23] (As the global climate change movement shows, it is not so easy in practice to draw a bright line between them.)

Others take a different view. Corey Robin wonders whether we can fight effectively against the sources of fear without having something to fight for. A healthy liberal democracy cannot do without positive goals, such as freedom, equality, and justice.[24] Reflecting this understanding, FDR and Winston Churchill, the drafters of the Atlantic Charter, incorporated ambitious (some would say utopian) postwar goals into their statement of war aims.

Nussbaum argues that hope is often a more effective motivator than fear. She offers a medical analogy: "The patient who is full of fear may become paralyzed; a hopeful patient may be more energetic in seeking solutions."[25] But there is an objection revealed by the "may." As Aristotle observes, fear can move us to deliberate about the best way of overcoming the source of the fear, but hope can lead to inaction, especially when it rests on faith. Zionists were not wrong to see faithful Jews' messianic hopes as the basis of an ultimately fatal passivity. Fear doesn't always paralyze, and hope doesn't always energize.

I end where I began. Fear is often a reasonable response to a genuine threat, but it can be a reaction to an imaginary threat. Demagogues exploit fear to gain power by pitting people against one another. Good leaders try to persuade people that they have agency and grounds for hope, even when the danger seems insurmountable.

Because we are vulnerable and mortal, we should not expect to live without fear. Because power-hungry individuals will always be among us, the exploitation of our fear is an ever-present possibility. Good institutions can reduce, but not eliminate, the risk that fear can lead us to trade liberty for security—and end up with neither.

The Rhetoric of Fear

Events can generate fear, but human decisions shape its consequences. Fear can be manipulated and often is. Ambitious leaders fan their followers' fears to increase their desire for security, which these leaders promise to supply at the cost of liberty. They can exaggerate the risks posed by specific groups or countries to boost support for policies needed to abate the alleged threat, including harsh treatment of ethnic, religious, and ideological groups suspected of collaborating with the country's enemies.

After the United States entered World War I, attacks on German Americans' language, culture, and physical safety intensified, and President Woodrow Wilson made it worse. "Any man who carries a hyphen about with him," he declared, "carries a dagger that he is ready to plunge into the vitals of this Republic when he gets ready."[26]

On the other hand, leaders can direct fear toward genuine threats, as Winston Churchill tried to do throughout the 1930s. Today, leaders across the political spectrum have converged on the conclusion that China represents a greater threat than was thought a decade ago, and most Americans have come to agree with them. History will judge whether this consensus was justified.

Preaching complacency entails risks, but so does sounding the alarm. When alarmists are mistaken, they can bring about the very conflict they warn against. Many critics of Americans' hardening attitudes toward China fear this outcome. The psychology of alarmism is seductive. It gives the alarmist a sense of superior insight, and by raising the stakes of one's judgment, it heightens the excitement. When leaders convey alarm to their followers, they enable ordinary citizens to feel a sense of significance that may otherwise be missing from their lives. But cures for boredom are often worse than the disease.

Leaders can intensify the prejudices and injustices that inevitably follow an enemy attack, or lean against them. In the aftermath of Pearl Harbor, many Americans and their leaders were convinced that Japanese Americans constituted a fifth column that would try to weaken the war effort against Japan. Although no evidence supported this belief, the governor of California, Earl Warren, echoed it, and President Franklin Roosevelt did nothing to resist it. The consequence was the unjustified internment of more than one hundred thousand American citizens for the duration of the war, and a Supreme Court decision, *Korematsu v. United States,* that ranks with *Dred Scott* and *Plessey v. Ferguson* as a black mark on U.S. jurisprudence.

Contrast this sorry episode with President George W. Bush's response to the 9/11 attacks. In the wake of these shocking events, it was plausible to believe that more would come—and to take steps at home and abroad to reduce the odds that they would. Nevertheless, President Bush worked hard to mute a public backlash against U.S. Muslims and prevent a repetition of the Japanese internment fiasco. He spoke out repeatedly against conflating American Muslims with the perpetrators of 9/11. In a speech at the Islamic Center in Washington, DC, he declared, "America counts millions of Muslims amongst our citizens, and Muslims make an incredibly valuable contribution to our country. . . . And they need to be treated with respect. In our anger and emotion, our fellow Americans must be treated with respect." The president took on directly those who sought to exploit the passions of the moment: "Those who feel like they can intimidate our fellow citizens to take out their anger don't represent the best of America, they represent the worst of humankind, and they should be ashamed of that kind of behavior."[27]

It is impossible to know whether President Bush's effort to reduce hate crimes against American Muslims made a difference, but the historical record suggests that it did. Although assaults against them rose in the immediate aftermath of the attacks, they quickly subsided. When leaders stand up against their supporters' worst instincts, they help to prevent fear from spiraling into hatred and violence. Americans have been lucky: the leaders we have had in moments of crisis—Washington, Lincoln, FDR, and others—have harbored no autocratic ambitions.

But we cannot hope to remain lucky forever. The antonym of fear is not love or even hope; it is courage. There is no substitute for the civic courage on which the defense of liberty always depends.

5 the drive for domination

I n the preface to *The City of God,* Augustine places the *libido dominandi*—the lust for domination—at the center of human existence. Residing in the hearts of all individuals, he writes, it explains collective phenomena such as imperialism, and is the purest manifestation of the self that cares only for itself— not for others, not for God. This self craves total control and recognizes no limits. It seeks to subject everything to its will, not just other human beings but also what counts as true or good.

The desire to dominate is unleashed by a sense of impunity, restrained by the fear of punishment, restricted by countervailing power. But it is purged, Augustine contends, only by the love of God. The inevitable result of our refusal to serve God is the desire to *be* God.

Not everyone can accept Augustine's insistence that we must reorient our souls toward a God whose existence many doubt and others reject outright. But it is possible to decouple Augustine's anthropology from his theology, as many great thinkers have done, including Thomas Hobbes and Friedrich Nietzsche. I will do so as well, because Augustine's account of domination helps us understand aspects of politics that are invisible or unintelligible without it.

The lust for domination is the desire for total power over an individual or a collectivity. Control through fear is not enough, because it leaves intact the possibility of invisible inward resistance, as in the German protest song "Die Gedanken sind frei" ("Thought Is Free"). The desire to dominate extends beyond bodies and actions to include the intellect and will. By the end of George Orwell's *1984*, Winston Smith "loved Big Brother" and accepted that 2 + 2 equaled 5.

Greek political philosophers understood tyranny as a means to constant pleasure (food, sex, luxury), or the limitless acquisition of wealth or honor. Analysts of modern tyranny focus on its ideological dimension—the striving to bend every aspect of society toward service to an extreme political vision, as Cambodia's Khmer Rouge sought to do. This aim can be pursued only when the defenders of the previous order have been rendered helpless to resist. By contrast, tyrants driven by the lust to dominate want total control for its own sake, a circumstance that offers a distinctive satisfaction linked to sadistic cruelty.

Two conditions make domination possible—the evisceration of institutional constraints, political or penal, and the absence of internalized restraints in those who seek it. There is nothing inside them—no principle, no sentiment, no social norm—that leans against their drive for absolute power. Once in office, leaders who seek such power begin by weakening and co-opting all institutions and centers of influence that could check their will. Independent judiciaries, a free press, opposition parties, fair elections, and protections for minorities are their first targets. But their goal is to free themselves from dependence on the will of others—the will of the majority in countries that retain the trappings of democracies, and the support of the ruling clique in those that do not. Leaders who seek domination employ the strategy of divide and rule, not only against their opponents but also against their supporters, as Stalin did in the 1930s and Xi Jinping is doing now.

The lust for domination is not the same as the desire for victory, because the worth of victory depends on the strength, not the weakness, of the opponent. Kansas City's victory in the 2023 Super Bowl over the Philadelphia Eagles was glorious because it was so hard-fought, because Jalen Hurt matched each of Patrick Mahomes's dazzling plays with one of his own.

Nor is the desire for domination necessarily linked to any of the dark passions—anger, hatred, humiliation, resentment, or fear. Leaders driven by the urge to dominate can arouse these passions among actual and potential supporters without experiencing them to the same degree (or at all). The soul of the potential dominator can be icy cold.

Domination is easily confused with other forms of craving for control, which can come from a place of weakness. Individuals can fight a feeling of internal chaos by trying to impose order on their environment. But some would-be tyrants gain a sense of strength and clarity of purpose from a singular focus on their dominant drive.

Nor is the *libido dominandi* the same as the desire for attention. Alice Roosevelt Longworth, Theodore Roosevelt's irrepressible daughter, once remarked that her father "always wanted to be the corpse at every funeral, the bride at every wedding and the baby at every christening."[1] But the desire for attention is fundamentally a stance of weakness; when you need the attention of others, they can dominate you. Their attention is a gift they can bestow or withhold.

Similarly, the desire to be recognized as meritorious or superior in some important respect is distinct from the drive to dominate. Among other differences, recognition is meaningless unless it is freely given. Verbal recognition elicited at the point of a gun may have instrumental value, as when hostages are forced to praise their captors and even to undergo religious conversion, but the gun-wielder can have no illusions about their sincerity.

This problem persists when asymmetries of power are less dramatic than between hostages and their captors. When individuals seeking recognition have the power to bestow benefits or impose burdens on others, insincere flattery is rational behavior for the less powerful, and the more powerful know this. Recognition matters only when it represents the sincere judgment of those whom the recognition-seeker regards as competent judges, a relationship that is incompatible with domination.

Nor, finally, is the lust for domination the same as the craving for fame. Unlike recognition, fame disregards differences among individuals. When the point is to be known by as many persons as possible, their competence to judge does not matter. But like attention and recognition, the pursuit of fame gives others extraordinary power over those who seek it. Attaining it may bring satisfaction, but fame is a species of dependence, not mastery.

Domination moves from the inside out, not the outside in. Dominators use a variety of tools and tactics to impose their will on the will of those they seek to control, whether individuals, small groups, or massive crowds.

Here are some examples of what I mean.

Early in 2023, a group of Memphis police beat Tyre Nichols until he was senseless. He died three days later. A few minutes into the encounter, which began with a traffic stop, it was evident that Nichols was entirely in the power of the police officers and incapable of resisting them. They kept beating him, even though their assault served no evident purpose. Why? Because he was in their power and unable to resist. Because they could. Even though their body cameras were turned on, they felt a sense of impunity, and they gave full rein to their desire to dominate another human being. If they had feared prosecution, they might have restrained themselves. But they allowed their darkest instinct to determine their conduct.

I do not know whether these young policemen enjoyed inflicting pain on their prisoner, but it is clear from the video that they were enjoying themselves. They seemed to be glorying in their unchecked power and in Nichols's total helplessness. That the experience of domination can be so satisfying is part of what makes it so dangerous.

This also seems to be the case in instances of prisoner mistreatment. While torture to obtain information is a purposive act whose means are shaped by its end, what the American guards did at Abu Ghraib was domination for its own sake. They reveled in it, grinning broadly as their colleagues photographed their deeds. They cannot have believed that what they were doing was terribly wrong—they saw it as misbehaving, perhaps, but surely not as a war crime or an atrocity. And they did not fear retribution. Otherwise, they would not have photographed themselves acting out their fantasies of domination.

Mobs expand the scope of this drive without changing its nature. They may begin with the desire for retribution against hated groups, as Kristallnacht did after the murder of a Nazi official by a desperate young Jew. But the frenzy feeds on itself as the mobs realize that they can do whatever they want with complete impunity. Cameras recorded crowds of Germans smiling as Jews were forced to clean streets with toothbrushes and Torah scrolls were hurled into bonfires. Police and firefighters called to the scenes of burning synagogues exerted themselves only to prevent the fires from spreading to non-Jewish-owned buildings. The dominant sentiment was no longer resentment or even hate but an overt glorying in total power over other human beings.

Speech can be a key tool in the pursuit of domination. Speakers who understand their craft can induce responses that their audiences do not and cannot resist. This ability can take benign forms; jokes evoke an involuntary reaction that when intense is termed "helpless" laughter. Many comedians are frank about their desire to dominate their audiences, as the vocabulary of their art reveals. When they deliver a strong performance, they are said to "kill" or "slay." Most of us, I suspect, enjoy the sense of telling a joke and evoking a roar of laughter. If my analysis is correct, this sentiment reflects our desire to exercise power over others, if only temporarily and with no intention of using this power for harmful ends.

Unscrupulous orators know how to exploit this drive by enabling people who feel weak individually to experience power collectively, and then to use this power to dominate the groups against whom the demagogue directs them. At the 1934 Nuremberg rally that Leni Riefenstahl memorialized in *Triumph of the Will,* Hitler addressed his phalanx of supporters, often rising to an apparent peak of passion. But as he paused to let the crowd respond, his face betrayed not passion but rather a cool satisfaction at his ability to dominate his listeners and to unleash their own drive to dominate others whom his regime had rendered weak and helpless.

Speech is how demagogues dominate, but there are other paths to unchecked power. Stalin was not a great orator, and neither is Xi Jinping. What distinguishes successful dominators is their ability to assess the power relations that define their situation, see possibilities that others do not, and subordinate all other considerations to the sole goal of increasing their power. They cannot let conventional norms of decency and humanity stand in their way. They must treat other individuals as means, not ends in themselves. Domination and objectification go hand in hand.

This linkage applies also to modern tyrants who treat domination as the prerequisite for the total remaking of society. The Khmer Rouge in Cambodia, for instance, developed an ideology that blended Maoism with xenophobic nationalism. To forge a society that promoted the rural peasantry over the urban proletariat, and dedication to the community over any form of personal interest, they employed a ruthless program of forced population transfer and mass murder that devastated their country. They treated their population as artists treat paint and sculptors marble—as raw materials to be shaped in accordance with their inner vision.

It is impossible to know whether these tyrants are truly dedicated to the ends they profess or whether their "ideals" cloak a drive to domination for its own sake. From the standpoint of humanity as an end in itself, it does not matter.

Augustine saw the *libido dominandi* as inherent in our sinful nature. Because we are all fallen, all sinners, it is a drive that grips us all. While this proposition has the virtue of theological consistency, it does not seem entirely true to the facts.

Politics and war are not the only arenas in which domination is manifested; it can pervade the most intimate relations. But some individuals seem satisfied to enjoy equal standing—to have a seat at the table, not to master it. Others are restrained by institutions, internalized norms, social disapproval, and the prospect of punishment. These suffice for most people in normal circumstances.

The threat of tyranny becomes real when individuals who are strongly driven to dominate are not sensitive to internalized restraints, and when the existing order has become weak enough to make a fundamental disruption possible. This often happens when substantial portions of a political community lose confidence that established institutions can meet their material needs, protect their security, and support their values. In a survey released in October 2016, 46 percent of Americans agreed that "because things have gotten so far off track in this country, we need a leader who is willing to break some rules if that's what it takes to set things right."[2] Against this backdrop, the results of the election a few weeks later become easier to understand.

Potential tyrants will always be among us, even in societies that profess to believe in the equal moral worth of human beings. In his Lyceum Address, delivered in 1838, the young Abraham Lincoln warned against the threat posed by individuals from the "family of the lion" or the "tribe of the eagle" whose drive for mastery was incompatible with the perpetuation of republican institutions. Lincoln had only one proposal to meet this threat—a system of civic education and a civic culture that inculcated such reverence for the Constitution and the laws that the people could be relied on to oppose would-be leaders driven by the desire to dominate.[3]

It has been a long time since an American leader has even tried to do this, and many elites focus more on the defects of the Constitution and the unequal application of the laws than on the prophylactic consequences of supporting them. History will judge whether this stance does more good—by promoting needed changes—than harm, by weakening the beliefs and institutions that are the only bulwark against overweening ambition.

Lincoln's Lyceum Address stands as a model of responsible political discourse. A young man without fame or power deployed the only tool he had—his capacity for translating deep reflection into compelling words—on behalf of institutions he believed in. The mature Lincoln understood that he had to dig deeper, to the principles undergirding these institutions and to the emotions that animate them, to preserve them for posterity—not unchanged, but reformed and founded anew.

Part III

Dark Passions and Democratic Rhetoric

6

politics as persuasive speech

Politics is flanked on the one side by economics, in which the core activity is exchange, and on the other by war, which employs force and threats backed by force in pursuit of some end. But politics fits poorly with both neighbors. Everyday moral sentiments suggest that there is something defective about agreements that are purely transactional or motivated by intimidation. The logic of corruption leaves something to be desired in politics, as does the language of the mobster. Distinctively political agreements rest on other motives and are achieved by other means. Of the three ways of coordinating disparate wills, persuasion is the most distinctively political.[1]

Political persuasion is in the service of action, not only belief. In representative democracies, each candidate vies to persuade voters that he or she is the best choice. But this is only part of the battle, and often not the hardest part; candidates must move their supporters to go to the polls and vote for them.

The gap between belief and action has been recognized since classical antiquity, as revealed in the proverbial contrast between two great Athenian orators. When Aeschines spoke, his listeners said, "How well he spoke." But when Demosthenes spoke, they said, "Let us march."

Voting is less demanding than fighting. But like every action, it comes with costs—time, energy, disruption of daily schedules. Candidates must persuade potential voters that casting their ballot is worth the cost.

To do this, candidates typically pursue a strategy of intensification. In a familiar trope, they will argue that "we have reached a critical crossroad" and "this is the most important election in our lifetime." The vices of opposing candidates and parties are caricatured or even invented, and the election becomes a Manichean battle between good and evil. Some candidates will even claim that it is the last chance to save what their audiences hold dear, as pro-Trump scholar Michael Anton did in his famous 2016 article "The Flight 93 Election."[2] The higher the apparent stakes, the more likely audiences will be to move from agreement with the speaker to the action the speaker urges.

When I watched a Trump rally for the first time, my first response was horrified fascination. But this quickly gave way to the realization that I was watching democratic politics in its purest form—a man using speech to mobilize a multitude to act as he wishes them to. Political insiders focus on polls, campaign structures, and get-out-the-vote drives. They have their place, as does mediated persuasion through advertising. But without a candidate who can speak persuasively to large audiences, these devices often fail.

Donald Trump did not conform to classical rhetorical canons. During his 2016 presidential campaign, he often said things that I was certain would destroy his candidacy. Instead, he showed me and other skeptics that the range of effective speech was broader than we had imagined. As someone familiar with the politics of the 1930s, I should not have needed this reminder. But like many others, I wrongly assumed that the bounds of effective speech had narrowed in modern America. It turns out that dangerous speech has not lost its power to persuade.

My second moment of discovery occurred on January 6, 2021, when a mob of Trump supporters invaded the U.S. Capitol in a failed effort to thwart the certification of Joe Biden as the duly elected president of the United States. More than a year earlier, I had drafted a philosophical essay with an imaginary example: suppose armed insurrectionists break into a country's legislature and threaten its members with dire consequences if they do not vote for constitutional change. The chair of the legislature bravely refuses and is shot dead on the spot, whereupon the remaining legislators hasten to comply. Now, as I watched on CNN, the scenario I had dreamed up to clarify the boundaries of politics was unfolding before my eyes. We will never know what would have happened if the mob had captured Vice President Mike Pence, whom they threatened to hang if he did not do President Trump's bidding.

Suppose they had found Mr. Pence and held a gun to his head to force him to exclude states with "contested slates" of electors from the Electoral College tabulation, allowing Donald Trump to retain the presidency. Although the insurrectionists would have achieved a political objective, it would not have been realized through political means.

Politics often involves conflict, but it is not war. The use of force to produce binding decisions for a political association is not politics but the failure of politics. Civil war is not politics; it is the collapse of politics. How can we see these forms of violence except as proof that political mechanisms for resolving disputes have broken down? Violence cannot be understood as the continuation of politics by other means, precisely because the domain of politics encodes a limitation on violence that is incompatible with war.

Classical Persuasion and Its Limits

My identification of persuasive speech as the core of politics is anything but novel. In classical antiquity, Greek philosophers took this proposition for granted, and it troubled them. Speech was a powerful weapon, they saw, but like all weapons, it could be used for destructive as well as worthy purposes.

The classic articulation of this concern occurs in a Platonic dialogue, the *Gorgias,* named for a renowned rhetorician who appears among the dramatic personae. At one, point, Gorgias tells the story of a patient whose doctor could not get him to follow the prescribed course of treatment. The doctor calls in Gorgias, who uses his persuasive powers to get the patient to comply. Although Socrates professes to be impressed, he soon points out that Gorgias knows nothing about medicine, and he worries about the consequences of a nonexpert having more power over the outcome than the expert. Suppose the orator chooses not to reinforce the doctor's judgment but to undermine it. Socrates would not have been surprised that contemporary injunctions to "follow the science" have proved ineffective in the face of appeals to public passions.

Later in the dialogue, Socrates considers the case of two speakers, one urging a difficult course of action requiring sacrifice to achieve a long-term good, the other claiming that an easier course would yield good results without any sacrifice at all. Most listeners would incline toward the latter speaker, whose popularity would rise. The former speaker, whom Socrates compares to a doctor counseling an unpleasant but necessary operation, wouldn't have a chance. "If a pastry baker and a doctor had to compete in front of children, or in front of men just as foolish as children, to determine which of the two, the doctor or the pastry baker, had expert knowledge of [healthy and unhealthy food], the doctor would die of starvation."[3]

The advocate of the undemanding course may genuinely believe sacrifice is unnecessary, in which case he is ignorant but not evil, or he may know that tough measures are needed but say the opposite to gain political power. In both cases, the long-term public good is undermined by an appeal to the public's short-term interests. In practice, the harder course prevails only when competitors for power unite to support it—or when events such as natural disaster, economic depression, or an enemy attack leave no other choice.

This appeal to short-term desires, Socrates adds, is a species of flattery. The speaker does not challenge the people; he praises them as virtuous and wise, not because he believes them to be so but to manipulate them into increasing his power. (Today's authoritarian populism, which castigates "corrupt" elites while praising the masses as virtuous, is only the latest example of this venerable practice.) Exasperated beyond endurance, Polus, an impulsive young student of Gorgias, offers a rejoinder: "Really? Don't they, like tyrants, put to death anyone they want, and confiscate the property and banish from their cities anyone they see fit?"[4] In response, Socrates forces his interlocutor to agree that tyrannical behavior is bad for the tyrant's soul.

Polus is silenced but not convinced, and neither are Plato's readers. The desire to dominate and punish others is part of human nature, and no amount of moral suasion will remove it from the souls of those whose ambitions are incompatible with institutional restraints and the rule of law. The ability to put persuasive speech in the service of domination has been, and remains, the greatest threat to democracies.

At its most dangerous, oratory appeals not to people's interests but to their passions. Socrates admits that he has angered many Athenians and that if he were hauled into court, he would have difficulty defending himself against their charges. He has led young people to ask questions their elders find offensive, and he has criticized political leaders he believes have led their city astray. Good intentions and sound advice are no defense against public ire, and orators who know their audience will have no trouble focusing its passions on alleged wrongdoers, whatever their actual culpability. Talented but amoral speakers can leave a trail of destruction in their wake—all the more so when they not only manipulate but also share their audience's passions.

In Aristotle's classic analysis, there are three sources of persuasion. The first rests on the character of the persuader: because so-and-so is well known for good judgment, virtue, and caring about those he addresses, he or she can be trusted to act effectively and in good faith to benefit those he seeks to persuade. Conversely, people will not heed the advice of someone who manifestly lacks these attributes. (As far as I can see, Aristotle does not address the problem posed by speakers who successfully pretend to have them but do not.)

The second form of persuasion relies on evidence and argument to carry the day, even when the evidence is inconclusive and the logic less than compelling. This is almost always the case in practical life, where evidence drawn from the past always risks getting the future wrong. For this reason, even the most solid political argument runs up against the inherent uncertainty of action in the world. We do not deliberate about mathematical proofs or scientific truths, but we can and do argue about the consequences they entail—for example, what we should do in response to the finding that climate change is real and affected by human activity.

The third form of persuasion rests on the speaker's ability to evoke passions and emotions in the audience. The ability to create, through words alone, sentiments such as hope, fear, confidence, anger, pity, indignation, envy, shame, even nostalgia for a better past, can mobilize listeners to support a course of action.[5]

This Aristotelean triad helps us understand what is distinctive about our own time. We see, first, that public and private virtue is no longer a necessary condition for trust. If candidates for public office can show that they want what their audiences want and are prepared to fight for it, the people will accept large deviations from standard norms of good character. The public expression of bad character can even be presented as proof of authenticity and a willingness to do whatever it takes to get results.

After the 2016 election, I asked a leading evangelical Protestant why so many evangelical voters had abandoned their long-held conviction that private morality is a threshold qualification for public office. His response: because evangelicals believed they were on the verge of losing every vestige of the culture they cherished, they were looking for a fighter, not a preacher. When people feel their backs are against the wall, they are unlikely to be particular about the character of those who step forward to defend them.

Another Aristotelean dimension of character—good practical judgment—also seems less important. In more normal times, evidence that one has performed well in politics is considered a sign of fitness for higher office. Today, the opposite seems more compelling. "Career politician" has become an epithet, and the candidate who enters politics from the outside has the advantage.

This inversion has strengthened a claim that recurs episodically in American history: because I made a fortune in business, I know how to run government—that is, like a successful business. If the skills needed to run a business were the same as those needed to govern effectively, this would be a reasonable argument. But they aren't. Nor are the skills needed to lead an army in battle. A business or military leader who is also good at governance (Michael Bloomberg, Dwight Eisenhower) occasionally emerges. But leaders of this sort succeed only because they understand the difference between their former and current professions.

In the fall of 2015, I attended a speech Donald Trump delivered, not at a rally but at a meeting in New Hampshire attended by independents as well voters from both parties. The centerpiece of his speech was a story he often told: after spending six years and millions of dollars trying and failing to renovate the skating rink in Central Park, New York City accepted Trump's offer to take over the construction in return for the right to run the rink. He completed the project ahead of schedule and under budget. Therefore, he claimed, he had what it took to run the government of the United States.

Trump succeeded in renovating the rink because he had total control of both his business and the project. But in our constitutional system, no one has this unlimited authority, and efforts to get it inevitably strain constitutional bounds. Government is not a business, and certainly not a family business, except in autocracies run by kleptocrats.

When prudence and virtue are no longer prerequisites, we are left with only one of Aristotle's pillars for trustworthy speakers: care for the well-being of their audience. This is where the rhetoric of identification is most powerful: I believe what you believe, I feel what you feel, I want what you want. I am you, my audience. I am your champion and your voice. There is only one difference between us: I have, or can get, the power you lack to make your dream a reality.

But why should your audience believe you? Credibility flows from consistency. If you stand your ground in the face of attack and are willing to endure the opprobrium of your adversaries, you demonstrate your commitment to the cause.

The truncation of trust in our time coincides with the diminished role of persuasion through logic and evidence. Partisan polarization is part of the reason: to the extent that partisan affiliation shapes citizens' views, the space for persuasion narrows. Also at work is the much-discussed splitting of Americans into different epistemic communities with distinctive beliefs about what is true and false. Absent shared frames of reference and a commonly acknowledged pool of facts among citizens, rational persuasion collapses. The pathologies of our time—the selective suppression of information, the deliberate creation of conspiracy theories, the dissemination of outright lies—make a bad situation worse. We are relearning the sad lesson of the years between the two world wars: no matter the truth of the claim, repetition can be the mother of persuasion.

Granted, some aspects of rational persuasion survive. One is the use of powerful examples to make one's case. Hearers are invited to conclude that a small part represents a larger whole. The appeal is qualitative, not quantitative; synecdoche almost always beats statistics. Effective political speech is usually concrete, and in the potency of specificity, akin to poetry.

Speakers also try to shape the agenda to their advantage by persuading their listeners that among the issues they care about, some are more important than they had previously believed. In Virginia's 2021 gubernatorial contest, for example, the Republican candidate, Glenn Youngkin, successfully intensified voters' concerns about public schools. A majority of these voters ended up voting for him, reversing the Democrats' traditional edge on this issue.

Finally, we see vestiges of rational persuasion in the use of narrative to clarify what voters find confusing and troubling. These stories have a basic structure: we're in a situation we don't like. Here's how we got here, and here's how we get to a better place. Successful narratives replace confusion with clarity, identify the wrongdoers, and chart an easily understood path forward.

Donald Trump's 2016 campaign was a classic of this genre. You're being marginalized economically and culturally, he told his audiences. Why? Because immigrants are pouring across our southern border, globalists are shipping jobs overseas, and elites are imposing their moral preferences on the rest of us. The solution: build a wall and deport people who don't belong here; pull out of one-sided trade treaties and bring the jobs home; and take control of the courts, the main institution through which the Left controls the culture.

As trust is debased and rational argumentation weakened, the third dimension of Aristotelean persuasion—the appeal to passions and emotions—comes to the fore.

Speakers can persuade by accurately assessing their audience's mood. Nearly four decades ago, while serving as the policy director for Walter Mondale's presidential campaign, I experienced an especially effective example of this phenomenon—Ronald Reagan's "Morning in America" television advertisement. As bucolic scenes of small-town America unfolded on the screen, a firm but comforting bass voice recited the gains from lower inflation the American people were enjoying under the president who had defeated

Jimmy Carter and then asked a killer question: why would we ever want to go back to the way things were before?

This ad worked because it appealed to many Americans' feelings of relief that after years when events seemed out of control, the country seemed to be recovering. If the Carter campaign had aired this ad four years earlier, it would have generated incredulity. If the Reagan campaign had unveiled it in early 1983 when the president's approval had bottomed out at 35 percent, it would have flopped. But by the spring of 1984, its appeal was irresistible.

Would-be leaders succeed in mobilizing the passions and emotions by crystalizing the unarticulated sentiments of their audience. They know they are succeeding when heads start nodding as they speak, and audiences start saying "Yeah" and "Damn right." Giving voice to these sentiments both confirms audiences in the correctness of their feelings and fortifies their connection with the speaker.

When speakers say what audiences privately believe but don't dare utter, the results can be explosive. Repression of speech creates an inner tension and also resentment toward those who claim the authority to distinguish between what we are permitted and forbidden to say. Politicians who deliberately cross this line are akin to stand-up comedians who, by saying the unsayable, unleash the repressed. Leaders who end the inner tension of forbidden thoughts and confirm their public legitimacy enjoy the gratitude of those they have liberated.

By doing this in public, moreover, speakers can forge communities of sentiment. Isolated individuals discover that they are not alone. Discovering one another through their shared response to the speaker strengthens their sentiment and confirms its legitimacy, and their sense of isolation and weakness is replaced by mutual empowerment. In mass politics, rhetoricians who can turn disconnected individuals into manifest communities with a collective purpose are enormously powerful.

7

how political speech can arouse—or tame— the dark passions

The dark passions are always with us, but they do not always dominate our social and political life. Circumstances matter, and so do leaders' responses to them. In times of peace and domestic tranquility, fears abate. In times of shared prosperity, gains for some do not come at the expense of others, leading to fewer occasions for resentment.

The circumstances that arouse or soothe the dark passions are shaped by the collective choices we make. In recent decades, for example, our economic policies benefited some regions of the United States but allowed others to fall behind. Worse, our leaders seemed indifferent to the pain of those who were losing out. By conveying the sense that some citizens mattered more than others, this indifference added the humiliation of invisibility to the pain of loss.

The response to the financial crisis and the Great Recession made matters worse. The bailout of the country's largest banks may have been necessary, but it appeared unjust at a time when millions of Americans were losing their jobs and homes without protection or compensation. Business leaders whose cavalier risk-taking helped precipitate the crisis kept their jobs and their seven-figure bonuses.

The people who continued to prosper in hard times seemed to look down on those who were struggling. They saw themselves as winners in the new economy's meritocratic competition. They had worked hard to get college degrees and advanced training, and now they were reaping the rewards. Others, who could have done the same and chose not to, refused to accept responsibility and instead blamed the winners for their plight. While campaigning in Pennsylvania in 2008, Barack Obama argued that as the economic losers become embittered, "they cling to guns or religion or antipathy toward people who aren't like them or anti-immigrant sentiment or anti-trade sentiment as a way to explain their frustrations." Eight years later, Hillary Clinton described many of Donald Trump's supporters as a "basket of deplorables."[1]

During these years, millions of Americans who experienced anger, humiliation, resentment, and fear struggled to express these sentiments in public life. As almost always happens, it took public speech to mobilize these passions and send them into battle. In this genre of rhetoric, effective speakers understand their audience's sentiments (often because they share them) and give them voice. The goal is not to persuade but to express what their audience already believes. In so doing, speakers make their audience feel heard, understood, and respected, and help legitimate what their audience believes. Speakers also can give their listeners a sense of liberation from constraint by saying the unsayable.

A bond of trust is forged between the speaker and the audience. "I am your voice" means "I speak on your behalf, not my own. Our deepest feelings coincide, and so do our goals. I will not betray you the way other politicians do, because serving my own interests means serving yours. If I win, you will too." This bond involves not only shared interest, but also shared identity. As a Trump supporter remarked, "What they hate about him is what they hate about me."[2]

Donald Trump's speech to the Conservative Political Action Conference (CPAC) in March 2023 offered a master class in the mobilization of dark passions to advance a political agenda. The former president began by evoking a threat to our continued existence as a nation. There are, he said, "sinister forces trying to kill America" by turning the country into a "socialist dumping ground for criminals, junkies, Marxists, thugs, radicals, and dangerous refugees that no other country wants."[3]

Some of these sinister forces were foreign countries that were "emptying out their prisons, insane asylums, and mental institutions and sending all of their problems right into their dumping ground, the USA." But other forces were domestic, including the establishment of his own party. "When we started this journey" in 2015, Trump declared, "we had a Republican Party that was ruled by freaks, neocons, globalists, open border zealots, and fools." The plot to ship undesirables across our border was abetted by immigration sympathizers like the Bushes, and by a self-interested business community that was also eager to ship American jobs overseas in pursuit of higher profits.

While some Republicans were well-intentioned "fools," Trump continued, the members of the other party knew exactly what they were doing. "From the beginning, we have been attacked by a sick and sinister opposition, the radical left communists, the bureaucrats, the fake news media, the big money special interests, the corrupt Democrat prosecutors." They are not just trying to destroy me; they are trying to silence you. We are in this together.

Fear can immobilize those who feel threatened or panic them into retreat. The only way we can save ourselves, Trump warned, is to fight back. "This is the final battle," he declared. "Either they win or we win. And if they win, we no longer have a country."

This fight is not only a response to a dire threat; it is fueled by deep resentment. "In 2016, I declared [that] I am your voice," Trump reminded his audience. "Today I add, I am your warrior, I am your justice. And for those who have been wronged and betrayed, I am your retribution."

The distinction between justice and retribution is key. Justice can be governed by reason and guided by law, but retribution is ungoverned and lawless. This resonant word, *retribution,* distills what happens when dark passions are unleashed. Passionate speech addressed to crowds can give individuals who feel powerless and trapped a sense of collective strength and possibility. This power of speech can be used for good purposes, but when it weakens the restraints that allow societies to function despite internal differences, reason loses its power, and chaos ensues.

After Marc Antony has persuaded the assembled Romans that the assassination of Julius Caesar was an attack on them as well, a mob surges into the streets to take revenge on the conspirators. When they encounter a man who shares a name with one of the assassins, he protests that he is Cinna the poet, not Cinna the conspirator. "Kill him for his bad verses," cries a member of the mob. And they do.

Because you have been wronged, victory is not enough; the vanquished must be punished for their wrongdoing. Here is how Trump described what victory means: "With you at my side, we will demolish the deep state. We will expel the warmongers. We will drive out the globalists, we will cast out the communists, we will throw off the political class that hates our country."

The verbs in these sentences—*demolish, expel, drive out, cast out, throw off*—convey a single message: the forces we will defeat are not fellow citizens with a different conception of what best serves our country. They have wronged us because they hate our country. They are the enemies of the people. They must pay for what they have done to us and to our country, and we must make sure they can never do it again.

Permanently crushing your enemies means dominating them, and domination knows no limits. If your defeated adversary tries to stand up, kneel on him until he abandons the effort. Better still, put such fear into your enemies that they don't even try to resist.

In war, soldiers often come to see their adversaries as less than human. Much the same happens when the line between politics and war disappears. One Trump supporter put it this way: "I'm not voting for him to be my pastor; I'm voting for him to be my president. If I have rats in my basement, I'm going to try to find the best rat killer out there. I don't care if he's ugly or if he's sociable."[4] If your enemies are rats, you don't try to persuade them to leave your basement; you use what works best to eradicate them.

As I listened to Donald Trump's speech to the CPAC, my mind drifted to a book I encountered long ago, Richard Hofstadter's *The Progressive Historians.* Toward the end, the author reflects on the fundamental requirement of a decent society, the outlook he calls "comity."

> Comity exists in a society to the degree that those enlisted in its contending interests have a basic minimal regard for each other: one party or interest seeks the defeat of an opposing interest on matters of policy, but at the same time seeks to avoid crushing the opposition, denying the legitimacy of its existence or values, or inflicting upon it extreme and gratuitous humiliations beyond the substance of the gains that are being sought. The basic humanity is not forgotten; civility is not abandoned; the sense that a community life must be carried on after the acerbic issues of the moment have been fought over and won is seldom far out of sight; an awareness that the opposition will someday be the government is always present.[5]

When the dark passions dominate politics and social relations, comity erodes, and enmity, vengeance, domination, and dehumanization come to the fore. Decency is thrown on the defensive, and liberal democracy—which, more than any other form of government, requires restraint and mutual forbearance—becomes hard to sustain.

The Founders were not naïve. They knew that the dark passions cannot be eradicated, only restrained. "Why has government been instituted at all?" Alexander Hamilton asks in Federalist 15. "Because the passions of men will not conform to the dictates of reason and justice, without constraint." The men who designed the Constitution understood that when these passions escape restraint, the likely consequence is tyranny, the greatest of all political ills. Institutions that disperse power, they believed, offer the best check on the tyrannical lust for power and domination.

The best check, but not a perfect one. The character of the people matters, and so does the conduct of leaders. When circumstances make large numbers of citizens angry, fearful, and impatient, an opening is created for unscrupulous individuals to seek power by appealing to the darkest impulses of our nature, using speech as a weapon against order and decency. No institutions have been devised to guarantee against this danger, and I doubt that any ever will be.

It is not my intention to denigrate any of the strategies that liberal democracies employ to strengthen themselves against the forces seeking to undermine them. Ameliorative policies matter, and so do institutional reforms. It would be naïve to believe that responsible speech is a sufficient cure for the pathologies that irresponsible speech exacerbates. Nonetheless, speech that can soothe our fears and tame our destructive impulses is indispensable.

Because it is better to anticipate and ward off threats than to counter them after they have emerged, leaders should understand the long-term consequences of acting on temporary passions and short-term interests. After four years of bloodshed in the First World War, the victors sought revenge against the vanquished. The key result was the Treaty of Versailles, which required Germany to accept full responsibility for starting the war and for its destructive consequences. Germany was forced to disarm, make territorial concessions, and pay reparations in ruinous amounts.

Some observers, including the economist John Maynard Keynes, argued that the treaty's demands were excessive, but their warnings went unheard. Although historians debate the extent to which the treaty contributed to the outbreak of World War II, even a cursory study of Hitler's prewar rhetoric shows how effectively he used Germans' sense of unjust treatment to evoke sentiments of humiliation and resentment and forge them into burning anger.

Heedlessness can be as damaging as malice. During the first decade of the twenty-first century, the United States lost more than 5 million manufacturing jobs. Technological change was partly to blame, but so too was the decision—backed by leaders of both parties—to admit China to the World Trade Organization on terms that gave it an advantage over established industrial powers. The disappearance of these jobs devastated many small towns and rural communities where manufacturing plants that had sustained them for generations shut their doors, leaving the people in these areas with no place to turn.

The speeches given by presidents and leaders of both parties seldom referred to this development, and no policy responses commensurate with the problems were ever proposed. Understandably, those who suffered the most felt voiceless and—even worse—invisible.

Sustained neglect of a group's legitimate complaints fosters resentment, and verbal signs of disrespect make it worse. Made public, the ill-considered words of presidential candidates Obama and Clinton reinforced the belief that these leaders did not respect a substantial portion of the citizenry. Anger joined resentment to create a combustible combination of dark passions, clearing the way for an orator prepared to channel these passions for his own purposes. Like nature, politics abhors a vacuum, and such a man arose to fill it.

Once leaders realize that they are facing dark passions, they should do what they honorably can to alter the forces, whether material or rhetorical, that have evoked them. This is an inherently difficult task. Concrete programs may not fully convince angry citizens that they are being heard, and respectful words may not persuade resentful audiences that their leaders view them as equals. But such responses can help reduce the intensity of destructive sentiments.

So can publicly apologizing and frankly accepting responsibility for what has gone wrong. In the wake of the brutal Hamas attack of October 7, 2023, most Israeli military and intelligence leaders did both. But Prime Minister Netanyahu did neither, enraging a people grappling with grief and fear and destroying what remained of their trust in him.

On the eve of the Normandy invasion, General Dwight Eisenhower prepared two speeches, one for victory, the other for defeat. The speech he never had to give read as follows:

> Our landings in the Cherbourg-Havre area have failed to gain a satisfactory foothold and I have withdrawn the troops. My decision to attack at this time and place was based on the best information available. The troops, the air and the Navy did all that bravery and devotion to duty could do. If any blame or fault attaches to the attempt it is mine alone.[6]

These are the words of a leader who understood his responsibilities to those he led—and to the institutions within which he acted, which cannot endure without public trust. He did not seek to evade or minimize the reversal his troops might have suffered, or shift the blame to others. Today's leaders should emulate him, but they rarely do.

Speech that accepts responsibility is one way leaders can build trust. Another way is by shaping their speech to explain and justify their proposals. Rhetoric that draws listeners in by appealing to their capacity for understanding the source of the problems they face and treating them as adults who can be part of the solution is likely to be more effective than appeals to expertise or authority. As we learned during the pandemic, "Follow the science" will not persuade those who do not understand the science and fear that it is being used as an instrument of coercion. It makes matters worse when corrigible scientific findings are presented as settled truths—or when leaders fail to distinguish between these findings and their consequence for political practice, which is inherently contestable.

Times change, of course, and the rhetorical choices that work in one situation may fall flat in another. Still, it is instructive to examine past examples of effective speech.

Countering Fear

FDR delivered his first "Fireside Chat" on March 12, 1933, the tenth day of his presidency. It is a classic of explanatory rhetoric. The president began simply: "I want to talk with the people of the United States about banking."[7] He distinguished between the few Americans who understand the mechanics of the banking system and the "overwhelming majority" who rely on the system without needing to understand it. Now that his administration had declared a bank "holiday" on March 6 and was preparing to reopen them on the 13th, he said, everyone needed to grasp the basics in order to have confidence in the steps the new administration had taken.

FDR proceeded to explain, in ordinary language, the basics of banking. Most of the money citizens deposit is lent out "to keep the wheels of industry and of agriculture turning." The banks retain only a small part of their deposits to cover withdrawals. In ordinary times, this reserve is more than enough. But when people lose confidence and rush to withdraw their savings, banks cannot repay all the depositors at once, and they either close their doors or fail. This was the situation the new president faced when he took office on March 4, 1933.

FDR then laid out the steps he had taken to restore the soundness of the banking system and permit the banks to reopen. He told his listeners that the banks would reopen in phases, not all at once, and he reassured them by anticipating a concern: banks that reopened later were just as sound as those that reopened on the first day. Even banks that needed to be reorganized before reopening would be sound when they did.

Throughout his chat, FDR recognized the dominant sentiment of his listeners—fear born of uncertainty—and he addressed it head-on. "When the people find that they can get their money—that they can get it when they want it for all legitimate purposes—the phantom of fear will soon be laid [to rest.]" He concluded this portion of his remarks by quipping, "I can assure you that it is safer to keep your money in a reopened bank than under the mattress."

FDR understood that the American people wanted to know why this financial crisis had occurred. He resisted the temptation to demonize bankers. A few had behaved incompetently or dishonestly, but the vast majority had not. They had gotten trapped in a situation not of their making. The free market could not handle the ensuing crisis unaided, which is why it fell to the government to straighten out this situation and to do it as quickly as possible.

The president did not make the mistake of overpromising: some banks would not reopen, and some individuals would suffer losses. The point of his program was to minimize the damage while restoring public confidence.

In his peroration, FDR transmuted the restoration of confidence into a shared national project. There is an element of banking reform, he said, that is "more important than currency, more important than gold, and that is the confidence of the people." And then he subtly raised the stakes: "Confidence *and courage* are the essentials of success in carrying out our plan" (my italics). Reengaging with the banking system, he implied, was a chance to display fortitude in the face of danger. It was an act of civic virtue. Returning to the famous theme of his first inaugural, he concluded by rallying his fellow citizens to their common task: "Let us unite in banishing fear."

FDR's tone was calm, unifying, and inspiring. The appeal was to reason, common sense, and civic virtue. Perhaps most important, the president treated his listeners as fellow citizens capable of agency, not as the passive subjects of public policy. The word *chat* connoted an informal conversation among equals, and *fireside* suggested people sitting together at the same level, not an audience facing an elevated lectern. In sum, the tone, content, and setting of the president's remarks were designed to treat people as equals, and by doing so to convey respect.

Soothing Anger

From time to time in American history, our leaders have appealed to the "better angels of our nature." It has not always worked. Not long after Abraham Lincoln concluded his first inaugural with this phrase, the Civil War began. In times of uncertainly and strife, the darkness within us often prevails.

But not always.

Upon landing in Indianapolis for a campaign event on April 4, 1968, Senator Robert F. Kennedy was informed of Martin Luther King Jr.'s assassination. He took it upon himself to convey this news to his mostly Black audience, knowing what the initial reaction would be. "You can be filled," he said, "with bitterness, with hatred, and . . . a desire for revenge."[8] This was understandable, but its consequences would be counterproductive—more violence and racial polarization.

There was another path, Kennedy reminded his listeners—that of the slain civil rights leader himself, who sought to replace the "stain of violence" with compassion and love, even as he led a great struggle for justice. This was not an impossible dream, Kennedy declared: "The vast majority of white people and the vast majority of black people in this country want to live together, want to improve the quality of our life, and want justice for all human beings who reside in our land." He urged his listeners to return home to pray for Martin Luther King's family and for the country. They disbanded without incident, and unlike hundreds of American cities, Indianapolis remained calm that night.

During his remarks, RFK invoked the memory of his assassinated brother to convey that he had felt—and continued to feel—the shock and bitterness his audience was feeling. This shared experience allowed him to express empathy in a manner that was received as genuine, and it gave him the standing to urge his audience to rise above their very human first reaction. He deployed his character, forged in tragedy, to strengthen his message. It is not clear that the same words from another political leader could have achieved the same effect.

The Strengths and Limits of Political Speech

Rhetoric is powerful in politics, but it is not omnipotent. President Lincoln, who delivered two of the greatest speeches in American history, acknowledged this. "I claim not to have controlled events," he said, "but confess plainly that events have controlled me."[9] His debates with Stephen Douglas, an unparalleled example of sustained public reasoning, did not suffice to earn him the Senate seat he sought.

Whatever the merits of their aims, politicians often fail, and we should not be surprised when they do; the gap between their good intentions and the desired political outcome is often too wide to bridge. Prejudice can be intractable, and passion some-times trumps reason. We cannot reasonably expect politicians to meet all the expectations they create to attain office. But we should expect them to minimize appeals to the darker side of our nature—and to the dangerous passions and drives that all too often lead to destruction.

We must "fight fire with fire," passionate advocates insist, and there is, I confess, an exhilarating sense of release when we do. But in the nonmetaphorical world, it is usually more effective to fight fire with water. Responsible leaders should seek to douse the flames and cool the temperature of our politics.

In constitutional democracies, restraints on speech are always suspect—nowhere more than in the United States. The only counterweight to bad speech is better speech that challenges the darkness within us in the name of our higher aspirations. The future of liberal democracy rests on the bet that these aspirations have not vanished from our souls.

This said, it is not my intention to substitute one naïveté for another. There are times when speech fails. Hatred cannot be appeased; it can only be opposed. Despots with imperial ambitions cannot be persuaded to set them aside; they can be thwarted only by force of arms or the threat of it. In such circumstances, relying on speech alone perpetuates illusions and evades hard choices.

The tug of war between liberal optimists and liberal realists has not ended and may never. Optimists can cite institutional and policy reforms that have improved social conditions and changed prevailing attitudes for the better. The danger, they argue, is that pessimism about human beings' capacity for change can lead us to aim too low, leaving remediable injustice intact and diminishing individuals' opportunity to lead more meaningful lives.

Realists need not reject these arguments, but they insist that institutional and policy reforms do not abate concerns about the dark side of human nature. Too often, liberal optimists are blindsided by ambitious leaders' ability to mobilize the public's anger, humiliation, resentment, fear, and desire to dominate, and to turn these qualities against liberal democracy itself. There is good reason to regard this challenge as perennial and to conduct politics accordingly. Progress is possible, but so is regression to ills we thought we had put behind us.

When backsliding is occurring, the most urgent challenge is to prevent things from getting worse. In such times, naïveté about historical progress and human nature is especially dangerous. Humans are capable of great goodness, but also great evil. While honorable leaders appeal to the better angels of our nature, others mobilize dark passions to exercise power without restraint. The capacity of institutions to protect us from these ills is limited.

I sense an objection: doesn't the emphasis on the power of speech in politics substitute a new form of liberal naïveté for the ones I have criticized? Aren't bribes and threats often more effective? Isn't the exclusion of exchange and force from the boundaries of politics a verbal trick that leaves the underlying problems as they were, unresolved?

My reply: everyone knows what exchange and force can accomplish. But too many leaders have overlooked the power of speech that addresses audiences as equals and fellow citizens, that explains the sources of our problems and makes the case that their proposals can ameliorate or even solve them. Then-president Barack Obama's droll proposal to appoint former president Bill Clinton as "Secretary of Explaining Stuff" was a bow to this neglected possibility.[10]

This is not the world of our dreams; it is the world in which we live. While public-spirited citizens and leaders must never abandon hope for the improvement of the human condition, their first duty is to see things as they are and act accordingly. We do not live in a world dominated by rational self-interest, let alone altruism or love. Political action can achieve its goals only when it is undertaken in full awareness of the threat the darker side of human nature will always pose.

notes

INTRODUCTION

1. For a useful argument in this vein, see Michael A. Neblo, "Philosophical Psychology with Political Intent," in *The Affect Effect: Dynamics of Emotion in Political Thinking and Behavior,* ed. W. Russell Neuman, George E. Marcus, Ann N. Crigler, and Michael MacKuen (Chicago: University of Chicago Press, 2007), 25–48. See also Raymond Geuss's essay "Thucydides, Nietzsche, and Williams," in his *Outside Ethics* (Princeton, NJ: Princeton University Press, 2005), 219–33.

2. I have in mind here Martha Nussbaum's *Political Emotions: Why Love Matters for Justice* (Cambridge, MA: Belknap Press of Harvard University Press, 2013). Although she repeatedly acknowledges the permanent presence of the dark passions in our nature, she is more confident than I am that liberal politics can generate and sustain a form of civic love that is strong enough to overcome them. A decade ago, she traced the fact that India was a "highly successful democracy" to the enduring influence of Gandhi and Tagore. In view of developments since then, especially the rise of religious passions and Narendra Modi's anti-liberal policies, she would probably want to revise this judgment. The dark passions have displaced civic love, not for the first time and surely not the last. More broadly, she seems to believe that politics

requires, and can be hospitable to, the emotions and connections that shape our private lives (p. 397). As a general proposition, I disagree, for the reasons Max Weber lays out at the end of his *Politics as a Vocation* (New York: Oxford University Press, 1946).

3. For a parallel approach written from a different theoretical and political stance, see Eva Illouz, *The Emotional Life of Populism* (Cambridge, UK: Polity, 2023).

4. For my earlier efforts to explore a nonreductionist approach to the passions, see William A. Galston, *Anti-Pluralism: The Populist Threat to Liberal Democracy* (New Haven, CT: Yale University Press, 2018), chapters 5–6; and Galston, "The Bitter Heartland," *American Purpose,* May 31, 2021.

CHAPTER ONE. THE MULTIPLE VULNERABILITIES OF LIBERAL DEMOCRACY

1. For a sympathetic account of these liberals, see Joshua Cherniss, *Liberalism in Dark Times: The Liberal Ethos in the Twentieth Century* (Princeton, NJ: Princeton University Press, 2023). For a decidedly less sympathetic account, see Samuel Moyn, *Liberalism Against Itself: Cold War Intellectuals and the Making of Our Times* (New Haven, CT: Yale University Press, 2023).

2. Freedom House, "Freedom in the World, 2023" (Washington, DC: March 2023), https://democratopia.info/wp-content/uploads/FIW_World_2023_DigitalPDF_compressed.pdf.

3. For apt comments on this form of government, see Jan-Werner Müller, *What Is Populism?* (Philadelphia: University of Pennsylvania Press, 2016), 49–57.

4. Avishai Margalit, *Of Compromise and Rotten Compromises* (Princeton, NJ: Princeton University Press, 2013).

5. Moyn, *Liberalism Against Itself,* 58.

6. John Stuart Mill, *On Liberty,* ed. David Spitz (New York: Norton, 1975), 56.

7. Reinhold Niebuhr, *Man's Nature and His Communities: Essays on the Dynamics and Enigmas of Man's Personal and Social Existence* (New York: Charles Scribner's Sons, 1965), 24.

8. John F. Kennedy, "Commencement Address at Yale University, June 11, 1962," John F. Kennedy Presidential Library and Museum, https://www.jfklibrary.org/archives/other-resources/john-f-kennedy-speeches/yale-university-19620611. Through a quirk of history (my father was a Yale professor), I was present at this speech, the significance of which I did not appreciate until many decades later.

9. David A. Graham, "The Wrong Side of the 'Right Side of History,'" *Atlantic,* December 21, 2015.

10. David Sanger, *New Cold Wars* (New York: Crown, 2024), 52.

11. These seemingly obvious considerations did not deter one of the world's best-known philosophers from proposing Cherubino, a figure in Mozart's *Marriage of Figaro,* as the model liberal democratic citizen— even though "Make love, not war" might well have been his motto. See Nussbaum, *Political Emotions,* chapter 2. As Nussbaum makes clear, this means that liberal democratic men must learn (from women) to be more like women. Understandably, proposals along these lines have met a mixed reception.

CHAPTER TWO. LIBERALISM AND THE DARK PASSIONS

1. Noel Malcolm, "Thomas Hobbes: Liberal Illiberal," *Journal of the British Academy* 4 (2016): 113–36.

2. Thomas Hobbes, *Leviathan,* chapter 13.

3. Quoted in Albert Hirschman, *The Passions and the Interests: Political Arguments for Capitalism Before Its Triumph* (Princeton, NJ: Princeton University Press, 1977), 16.

4. Quoted in Hirschman, *The Passions and the Interests,* 60.

5. Voltaire, *Philosophical Dictionary, Part IV* (1764).

6. Quoted in Hirschman, *The Passions and the Interests,* 58.

7. For the most persuasive argument along these lines, see Benjamin M. Friedman, "The Moral Consequences of Economic Growth," https//:scholar.harvard.edu/files/bfriedman/files/the_moral_consequences_of_economic_growth.pdf.

8. Only one hundred people can be on the list of the world's hundred richest individuals—a consequential tautology.

9. For all the quotations cited in this passage and more, see Michael Ruhle, "From Pacificism to Nuclear Deterrence," *NATO Review,* January 14, 2019.

10. Quoted in Hirschman, *The Passions and the Interests,* 134.

11. For a memorable rendition of this tension, see Gustave Flaubert's *Madame Bovary.* By the end, the dissatisfied central character, the romantic Emma Bovary, brings ruin to her husband and dies a miserable death, while the Enlightenment rationalist—Monsieur Homais, the pharmacist—receives the Legion of Honor.

12. We should not have forgotten Tocqueville's warning that the desire for prosperity can lead peoples to disregard the importance of liberty. See Hirschman, *The Passions and the Interests,* 122–25.

13. Quoted and discussed in Hirschman, *The Passions and the Interests,* 106–7.

14. Rupert Brooke, "Peace," *Poetry,* April 1915. This is not to deny that more personal elements (including a failed romance) also shaped Brooke's words.

15. Lyndon B. Johnson, "Remarks at the University of Michigan," May 22, 1964, The American Presidency Project, https://presidency.ucsb.edu/documents/remarks-the-university-michigan.

16. For example, Reinhold Niebuhr—one of the deepest intellectual sources of Cold War liberalism—was an Augustinian New Dealer. Another seminal Cold War thinker, Arthur Schlesinger Jr., said this of him: "He persuaded me and many of my contemporaries that original

sin provides a far stronger foundation for freedom and self-government than [do] illusions about human perfectibility." "Forgetting Reinhold Niebuhr," *New York Times,* September 18, 2005.

CHAPTER THREE. ANGER, HUMILIATION, AND RESENTMENT

1. Nicholas A. Valentino et al., " 'Election Night's Alright for Fighting': The Role of Emotions in Political Participation," *Journal of Politics* 73, no. 1 (January 2011): 156–70. At the same time, anger (unlike fear and anxiety) tends to suppress the search for new information. See Nicholas A. Valentino et al., "Is a Worried Citizen a Good Citizen? Emotions, Political Information Seeking, and Learning via the Internet," *Political Psychology* 29, no. 2 (2008): 247–73. Anger yields what might be termed close-minded mobilization and is the enemy of deliberation.

2. "Address at Madison Square Garden, New York City," October 31, 1936, The American Presidency Project, https://www.presidency.ucsb.edu/documents/address-madison-square-garden-new-york-city-1.

3. Leo Strauss, *Liberalism Ancient and Modern* (New York: Basic Books, 1968), 226.

4. Xerxes instructed his men to say the following as they administered three hundred lashes: "You salt and bitter stream, your master lays this punishment upon you for injuring him, who never injured you." Herodotus, *The Histories,* trans. Aubrey de Selincourt (Edinburgh: Penguin Books, 1964), 429.

5. For example, see Avishai Margalit, *The Decent Society,* trans. Naomi Goldblum (Cambridge, MA: Harvard University Press, 1996); Daniel Statman, "Humiliation, Dignity and Self-Respect," *Philosophical Psychology* 13, no. 4 (2000): 523–40.

6. Frederick Schick, "On Humiliation," *Social Research* 64, no. 1 (Spring 1997): 134–35.

7. Schick, "On Humiliation."

8. Jennifer S. Goldman and Peter T. Coleman, "A Theoretical Understanding of How Emotions Fuel Intractable Conflict: The Case of Humiliation," March 26, 2005, http://www.humiliationstudies.org/documents/GoldmanNY05meetingRT2.pdf.

9. Evelin Lindner, *Making Enemies: Humiliation and International Conflict* (Westport, CT: Praeger, 2006), 4.

10. Lindner, *Making Enemies*, 117–18.

11. Margalit, *The Decent Society*, 9, 262.

12. Benedict de Spinoza, *Ethics* (London: Penguin Books, 1996), 84. Granted, ordinary language suggests the possibility of justified pride consistent with accurate self-assessment. A craftsman takes pride in his work; a less than diligent student is proud of her ability to buckle down and study. But these self-assessments are of particular activities, not the overall state of one's soul or character. This generalized pride typically reflects inadequate recognition of one's shortcomings.

13. William Shakespeare, *Hamlet,* 2.2. 519–20.

14. I owe this observation to Matt Sleat. There are traces of a similar sentiment in Judaism; for example, in the account of Rabbi Akiva's martyrdom at the hands of the Romans.

15. Doron Shultziner and Itai Rabinovici, "Human Dignity, Self-Worth, and Humiliation: A Comparative Legal-Psychological Approach," *Psychology, Public Policy, and Law* 18, no. 1 (2012): 111.

16. See also Lindner, *Making Enemies*, 171.

17. Booker T. Washington tells this story in *Up from Slavery* (New York: Doubleday, 1901), chapter 6.

18. For the link between anger and depression, see Fredric N. Busch, "Anger and Depression," *Advances in Psychiatric Treatment* 15 (2009): 271–78.

19. Donald C. Klein, "The Humiliation Dynamic: An Overview," *Journal of Primary Prevention* 12, no. 2 (1991): 108; summarizing the research of John C. Spores, *Running Amok* (Columbus: Ohio University Press, 1988).

20. Quoted in Miriam H. Marton, "Terrorism and Humiliation," September 1, 2005, http://www.humiliationstudies.org/documents/MartonBerlin05meeting1.pdf.

21. Quoted in Goldman and Coleman, "A Theoretical Understanding of How Emotions Fuel Intractable Conflict," 6.

22. Robert Harkavy, "Defeat, National Humiliation, and the Revenge Motif in International Politics," *International Politics* 37 (September 2000): 346.

23. "Winston Churchill's Speech at the Mansion House, 10 November 1942," Imperial War Museums, https://www.iwm.org.uk/collections/items/object/1030031903.

24. "Full Text of Putin's Speech on Crimea," *Prague Post,* March 19, 2014, praguepost.com/eu-news/37854-full-text-of-putin-s-speech-on-crimea.

25. William A. Callahan, "National Insecurities: Humiliation, Salvation, and Chinese Nationalism," *Alternatives* 29 (2004): 204.

26. Callahan, "National Insecurities," 214.

27. For an interesting analysis, see Roxanne L. Euben, "Humiliation and the Political Mobilization of Masculinity," *Political Theory* 43, no. 4 (2015): 500–532. Euben makes a strong argument that in the case of Islam, humiliation is often experienced and described as a form of emasculation—that is, as imposed restraints that impede the acts and deny the status appropriate to men. For the reasons set forth in this article, I do not believe that this account works generally, although there are certainly analogues in Putin's Russia.

28. A respected analyst of Iran argues, however, that the shah's overthrow had more to do with internal conflicts than external meddling. See Ray Takeyh, *The Last Shah: America, Iran, and the Fall of the Pahlavi Dynasty* (New Haven, CT: Yale University Press, 2022.)

29. The classic analysis of this phenomenon in democratic societies is Judith Shklar, *Ordinary Vices* (Cambridge, MA: Harvard University Press, 1984), chapter 3 ("What Is Wrong with Snobbery?"). See

especially her depiction of Jacksonian democrats' response to the aristo-cratic pretentions of wealthy Americans (107–14).

CHAPTER FOUR. FEAR AND ITS FAMILY

1. "The Only Thing We Have to Fear Is Fear Itself," https://teach inghistory.org/history-content/ask-a-historian/24468. Thoreau's journal entry of September 7, 1851, echoed Montaigne's essay "On Fear."

2. Although this quote has been widely attributed to Emerson and echoes sentiments found in his essay on courage, I have been unable to locate a direct source.

3. Alexis de Tocqueville, *Democracy in America,* vol. 2, part 4, chapter 6.

4. "Franklin D. Roosevelt's Last Message to the American People," remarks prepared to be delivered on April 13, 1945, Library of Congress, https://www.loc.gov/resource/rbpe.24204300/?st=text. FDR died on April 12.

5. Micah 4:4.

6. "President Franklin Roosevelt's Annual Message (Four Free-doms) to Congress (1941)," National Archives, https://www.archives.gov/milestone-documents/president-franklin-roosevelts-annual-mes sage-to-congress.

7. Franklin D. Roosevelt and Winston Churchill, "The Atlantic Charter: Declaration of Principles Issued by the President of the United States and the Prime Minister of the United Kingdom," August 14, 1941, North Atlantic Treaty Organization, https://www.nato.int/cps/en/natohq/official_texts_16912.htm.

8. Aristotle, *Rhetoric,* 1382a22.

9. Aristotle, *Nicomachean Ethics,* 1115b.

10. Aristotle, *Nicomachean Ethics,* 1115b.

11. Aristotle, *Rhetoric,* 1382a26.

12. Aristotle, *Rhetoric,* 1383a6.

13. Quoted in Corey Robin, *Fear: The History of a Political Idea* (New York: Oxford University Press, 2004), 178.

14. Aristotle, *Rhetoric,* 1383a18.

15. Alison Gopnik, "Who's Most Afraid to Die? A Surprise," *Wall Street Journal,* June 6, 2018.

16. Quoted in Frank Furedi, *How Fear Works: Culture of Fear in the 21st Century* (London: Bloomsbury Continuum, 2019), 31.

17. Martha Nussbaum, *The Monarchy of Fear: A Philosopher Looks at Our Political Crisis* (New York: Simon & Schuster, 2019), 205.

18. Nussbaum, *The Monarchy of Fear,* p. 29.

19. Churchill, *The Story of the Malakand Field Force* (London: Bloomsbury Academic, 2015). First published in 1898, the book is Churchill's account of his military experiences in what is now Pakistan.

20. Churchill, quoted in Alan Reiner, "Winston Churchill Quotes," https://word-counter.com/popular/winston-churchill-quotes/; Arendt, quoted in Furedi, *How Fear Works,* 257.

21. Quoted in Furedi, *How Fear Works,* 221.

22. Quoted in Alex Schulman, *Hobbes, Thomas, 1588–1679,* September 15, 2014, https://doi.org/10.1002/9781118474396.wbept0472.

23. Quoted in Furedi, *How Fear Works,* 165.

24. Robin, *Fear,* 252.

25. Nussbaum, *The Monarchy of Fear,* 205.

26. Robert Siegel and Art Silverman, "During World War I, U.S Government Propaganda Erased German Culture," NPR, April 7, 2017, https://www.npr.org/2017/04/07/523044253/during-world-war-i-u-s-government-propaganda-erased-german-culture.

27. President George W. Bush, "Islam Is Peace, Says President: Remarks by the President at Islamic Center of Washington, D.C.," September 17, 2001, The White House, https://georgewbush-whitehouse.archives.gov/news/releases/2001/09/20010917-11.html.

1. "Alice Roosevelt Longworth Quotes," https://www.azquotes.com/author/9023-Alice_Roosevelt_Longworth.

2. Robert P. Jones, Daniel Cox, Betsy Cooper, and Rachel Lienesch, "The Divide over America's Future: 1950 or 2050? Findings from the 2016 American Values Survey," Public Religion Research Institute, October 25, 2016, https://www.prri.org/wp-content/uploads/2016/10/PRRI-2016-American-Values-Survey.pdf.

3. Lincoln, "The Perpetuation of Our Political Institutions: Address Before the Young Men's Lyceum of Springfield, Illinois," January 27, 1838, Abraham Lincoln Online, https://www.abrahamlincolnonline.org/lincoln/speeches/lyceum.htm.

1. The fuller argument behind this paragraph is as follows. Politics involves the nonviolent coordination of multiple wills toward collective action. Many types of means can promote this objective. If the goal of coordination is preserving the status quo, then habit, unexamined belief, and risk aversion often suffice. If the intention is to change the status quo, there are three strategic options—exchange, threat, and persuasion.

Exchange means offering benefits to specific individuals in return for their agreement and support. Versions of this strategy include buying votes, earmarks for projects of special interest to specific legislators, and providing campaign funds or other forms of electoral assistance.

Threat means warning individuals that if they fail to support a specific course of action, they will be deprived of something they value. This strategy is always available because nearly all members of political communities, citizens as well as officials, enjoy some valued goods and opportunities that can in principle be taken away. During the years when Joseph McCarthy dominated American politics, suspected Communists were threatened with the loss of their jobs and livelihood if they refused to name or testify against their colleagues, and many yielded to this pressure.

There is a partial resemblance between exchange, which involves hope of gain, and threat, which involves fear of loss. But the differences between them are at least as important. Not only is there a well-established asymmetry between gain and loss, the latter being felt more acutely than the former, but also the strategy of threat imposes some costs on the threat-maker that exchange does not. The individual offering an exchange anticipates and accepts making good on his or her side of the bargain. In contrast, the person making the threat hopes not to carry it out. The point is to use fear of loss to obviate the need to impose loss.

2. Publius Decius Mus [Michael Anton], "The Flight 93 Election," *Claremont Review of Books,* September 5, 2016.

3. Plato, *Gorgias,* 464d.

4. Plato, *Gorgias,* 466b.

5. Aristotle, *Rhetoric,* book 2.

CHAPTER SEVEN. HOW POLITICAL SPEECH CAN
AROUSE—OR TAME—THE DARK PASSIONS

1. "Obama Angers Midwest Voters with Guns and Religion Remark," *Guardian,* April 14, 2008; Hillary Clinton, speech delivered on September 9, 2016, *Time,* September 10, 2016, https://time.com/4486502/hillary-clinton-basket-of-deplorables-transcript/.

2. Roderick P. Hart, *Trump and Us: What He Says and Why People Listen* (Cambridge, UK: Cambridge University Press, 2020), 81.

3. All quotations from Trump's speech are taken from "Trump Speaks at CPAC 2023 Transcript," Rev, https://www.rev.com/transcripts/trump-speaks-at-cpac-2023-transcript.

4. Hart, *Trump and Us,* 81.

5. Richard Hofstadter, *The Progressive Historians* (New York: Knopf, 1968), 454.

6. Scott Simon, "The Speech Eisenhower Never Gave on the Normandy Invasion," NPR, June 8, 2013, https://www.npr.org/2016/06/08/189535104/the-speech-eisenhower-never-gave-on-the-normandy-invasion.

7. "Fireside Chat on Banking," March 12, 1933, The American Presidency Project, https://www.presidency.ucsb.edu/documents/fireside-chat-banking.

8. "Full Text of Robert F. Kennedy's Speech: Indianapolis, April 4, 1968," Kennedy King Memorial Initiative, https://www.kennedyking indy.org/full-rfk-speech.

9. Lincoln, "Letter to Albert G. Hodges," April 4, 1864, The American Presidency Project, https://www.presidency.ucsb.edu/documents/letter-albert-g-hodges.

10. "Bill Clinton, Obama's New 'Secretary of Explaining Stuff,' Takes Show on Road," NPR, September 12, 2012, https:/www.npr.org/sections/itsallpolitics/2012/09/12/160995401/bill-clinton-obamas-new-secretary-of-explaining-stuff-takes-show-on-road.

acknowledgments

I recently read a book whose acknowledgments included expressions of gratitude to more than two hundred individuals. I was envious and astounded. Writing this book was a painfully solitary task, undertaken in the depth of the pandemic. I consulted no one until I completed a first draft, the inadequacies of which quickly became apparent. I began again, with the same result. It was not until the third draft that I had the argument in the sequence in which it now appears, after which a round of edits consumed the better part of another year.

All told, it took more than four years to produce the slender tome you are now perusing. Only now do I understand a remark of Pascal's I encountered as a graduate student, to the effect that he would have written a shorter letter if he had had more time.

Along the way, I incurred a handful of debts: to the Brookings Institution for giving me the freedom to wander off the beaten track; to my editor at Yale, William Frucht, for his candor, courtesy, and skillful management of this manuscript through the publication process from beginning to end; and most of all, to my colleague Jonathan Rauch for his wise council and unflagging support. He had more confidence in this venture than I did. I hope he is right.

I am grateful to *The American Purpose* and Columbia University Press for permission to adapt previously published material for new purposes.

Index

abolitionists, 15, 53

Abu Ghraib, mistreatment of prisoners at, 49, 55, 98

Aeschines, 106

Affordable Care Act of 2010, 45

alarmism, psychology of, 90

anarchy, 17, 28, 30

Angell, Norman, 33

anger: appeal to, 125; cognitive component of, 3; depression and, 142n18; dishonor and, 46; exploitation of, 91; fear and, 66, 127; frustration and, 3, 45, 120; harm-based, 45–46; hatred compared to, 44; humiliation and, 46–47, 53–55, 126; mobilization of, 43, 111, 120, 134, 141n1; persuasive speech and, 110, 111; politics of, 23, 36; resentment and, 62, 63, 66, 126–27; soothing, 131–32; sources of, 3, 45–47. See also dark passions

antipathy. See hatred

anti-Semitism, 44

Anton, Michael, 106

Arab nationalism, 60

Arab Spring, 47

Arendt, Hannah, 85

Aristotle, 17, 30, 61–62, 70–74, 88, 111–13, 115

Atlantic Charter (1941), 69, 88

Augustine (Saint), 2, 37, 93–94, 100

authoritarianism, 14, 17, 110

autocracy, 1, 2, 4, 13, 18, 91, 113

Balkan wars, 21, 34

Begin, Menachem, 61

Berg, Nicholas, 55

Berlin Wall, fall of (1989), 12, 21, 24

Beveridge Report (1942), 10

biases. See prejudice

Biden, Joe, 107

Bloomberg, Michael, 112

Boswell, James, 32

and, 17; of speech and thought, 22, 30; Tocqueville on, 17, 140n12; tyranny and, 16. *See also* civil rights and liberties
Freud, Sigmund, 21, 37
Frost, Robert, 4
frustration, 3, 14, 45, 55, 120
future, fear of, 45, 77–82

Gandhi, Mohandas, 137n2
genocide, 34, 44
George III (king of England), 30
German Americans, treatment during World War I, 89
Germany: national humiliation in, 23, 56–57; Nazism in, 44, 49, 57, 69, 98–99; territorial irredentism and, 56; Treaty of Versailles and, 23, 56–57, 125–26
Goldman, Jennifer, 49
Gorgias (Plato), 108–10
Great Depression, 67, 75
The Great Illusion (Angell), 33
Great Recession, 66, 119–20
Great Replacement narrative, 36
Great Society, 37–38
Green, T. H., 39
Gresham's law, 3

Hamas attack on Israel (2023), 44, 127
Hamilton, Alexander, 38–39, 124
Harkavy, Robert, 57
hatred: anger compared to, 44; hate crimes, 91; mobilization of, 43, 123; politics of, 4, 23, 36, 43; self-hatred, 51. *See also* dark passions
Havel, Václav, 54

Hegel, Georg Wilhelm Friedrich, 62
Herodotus, 45
Hinduism, 36
Hitler, Adolf, 37, 44–45, 99, 126
Hobbes, Thomas, 2, 27–31, 60, 62, 87, 94
Hofstadter, Richard, 124
Holocaust, 20–21, 37, 44
honor: acquisition of, 94; aristocratic, 35, 46; compromise and, 4; in defeat, 55–56; efforts to regain, 61; in Hobbes's political theory, 29, 87; as martial virtue, 35; politics of, 57, 62; tribal codes of, 52. *See also* dishonor
hope: commercial optimism and, 32, 33; constitutional order and, 1–2; fear in relation to, 68, 73–74, 76, 86, 88; in Hobbes's political theory, 28, 29; mobilization of, 111; persuasive speech and, 111; post–World War II liberalism and, 12; rhetoric in summoning of, 35–36; as source of inspiration, 3; transforming into confidence, 74
humiliation: anger and, 46–47, 53–55, 126; collective, 56–60; definitions of, 50–53; depression and, 54; description of, 47–50; exploitation of, 57, 58; mass shootings and, 54; mobilization of, 120, 134; national, 23, 36, 56–59; politics of, 23, 36, 55–61, 119; resentment and, 56, 57, 126; responses to, 53–54; self-interest and, 62; terrorism and, 54–55. *See also* dark passions

Hungary: illiberal democracy in, 13; national humiliation in, 23
Huntington's chorea, 77–78
hypochondriacs, 78

illiberal democracy, 13, 138n3 (ch.1)
immigrants, 18, 36, 45, 81, 115, 120, 121
India, religious issues in, 36, 137n2
Iran: as autocratic state, 13; British domination of oil industry in, 59; overthrow of Mosaddeq in, 60, 143n28; revolution in (1979), 60
Islam. *See* Muslims and Islam
Israel: Hamas attack on (2023), 44, 127; Six-Day War and (1967), 56, 60; Yom Kippur War and (1973), 61

Japanese Americans, internment during World War II, 90
Jews and Judaism: anti-Semitism and, 44; Holocaust and, 20–21, 37, 44; humiliation by Nazis, 49; Kristallnacht and, 98; martyrdom and, 142n14; in World War I, 44, 72; Zionists, 88
Johnson, Lyndon, 37–38
Johnson, Samuel, 32
Jonas, Hans, 87
justice: for all people, 131–32; government designed to promote, 124; as inspiration, 3; liberal democracy and, 88; politics of fear and, 87; retribution vs., 122

Kant, Immanuel, 24
Kennedy, John F., 21, 139n8

Kennedy, Robert F., 131–32
Keynes, John Maynard, 34, 126
Khmer Rouge, 94, 99–100
King, Martin Luther, Jr., 131–32
Korematsu v. United States (1944), 90

Lennon, John, 25
Letter on Toleration (Locke), 30
Leviathan (Hobbes), 28
liberal democracy: attacks on, 1, 10, 13, 66; Cherubino as model citizen in, 139n11; compromise in, 4, 15; core principles of, 9–10; defenders of, 1, 2, 11, 12, 18, 19, 23; duties and responsibilities of leaders in, 4; economic systems compatible with, 10; future of, 11, 38, 133–35; goals for society, 85, 87, 88; illusions regarding, 12, 13, 17–25, 133; institutional restraints and, 1, 9, 14; neoliberalism compared to, 9–10; power in, 9, 14, 16; strategies for strengthening, 125; threats to, 13, 17–18, 37, 110, 124; vulnerabilities of, 10–17
liberalism: in Cold War, 37–39, 140n16; cultural, 12; of fear, 38, 87; history of, 11–12, 138n1; Hobbes on, 27; idealist, 39; Locke on, 31; Moyn on, 16, 37; neoliberalism, 9–10, 39; of self-development, 38; social perfection and, 16–17. *See also* liberal democracy
Liberalism against Itself (Moyn), 37
liberal nationalism, 20
liberty. *See* civil rights and liberties; freedom

passions. *See* dark passions

Pearl Harbor attacks (1941), 90

Pence, Mike, 107

persuasive speech: for bolstering institutions, 4–5; in classical antiquity,
106, 108–11, 122–23; communities
of sentiment and, 116–17; dark passions and, 110, 111, 115, 116, 122–23;
drive for domination and, 98–99,
110, 123; forms of persuasion,
111–16; intensification strategy
for, 106; mob behavior and, 107,
122–23; mobilization through, 1,
105–7, 111, 122–23; politics and,
105–17, 132–35, 146n1; power and,
108–10, 113, 122; strength and limits of, 132–35. *See also* rhetoric

pessimism, 37–39, 133–34

Plato, 61, 108–10

police brutality, 97

political speech. *See* persuasive
speech; rhetoric

politics: of anger, 23, 36; aspirational, 23, 37, 39; of drive for domination, 23, 36, 100; emotions and,
2, 137–38n2; exchange as used
in, 105, 134, 146–47n1; expectations regarding, 4–5; failure of,
4, 108, 132–33; of fear, 23, 36, 82,
86–89; of hatred, 4, 23, 36, 43;
Hobbes's theory of, 27–31, 87;
of honor, 57, 62; of humiliation,
23, 36, 55–61, 119; liberal, 37–39,
137n2; passionate eruptions in,
3; persuasive speech and, 105–17,
132–35, 146n1; psychology of, 2,
23; of resentment, 23, 36, 62–64;

role in transforming hope into
confidence, 74; threats as used in,
105, 146–47n1; universal utilitarianism's inapplicability to, 20

Pope, Alexander, 74

populism, 18, 59–61, 110

poverty, 20, 22, 38, 80

power: absolute, 94; collective,
99; of culture, 18, 25; of dark
passions, 2; drive for domination
and, 93–99; institutional, 16, 125;
in liberal democracy, 9, 14, 16;
oppressive, 56; persuasive speech
and, 108–10, 113, 122; pursuit of,
1, 3–4, 29, 34, 38, 88; regulatory, 10; of religion, 18–19, 25; of
resentment, 64; of revenge, 23;
of rhetoric, 132, 134–35; for self-
reflection, 67; unchecked, 97, 99,
134; unequal relations of, 49, 63,
96. *See also* tyranny

precautionary principle, 79

prejudice: anti-Semitism, 44;
internalized, 51; intractability of,
133; Pearl Harbor attacks and, 90;
xenophobia, 99

pride, 11, 46, 47, 50–52, 57, 60–62,
142n12

prisoner mistreatment, 49, 55, 97–98

privacy, 3, 9, 81–82

The Progressive Historians (Hofstadter), 124

progressivism, 37, 39, 87

Psycho (film), 78

psychology: of alarmism, 90; in
commercial societies, 31; dyadic
vs. triadic, 2; of fear, 68, 71;

individual vs. group, 55; moral, 61–62; naïveté and, 23; pessimism and, 38; of politics, 2, 23

Putin, Vladimir, 21, 24, 36, 58, 143n27

Rabinovici, Itai, 53

rage. *See* anger

Reagan, Ronald, 115–16

realism, 2, 13, 25, 35, 37–39, 57, 69, 133–35

reason: appeal to, 130; in courts of law, 3; in Hobbes's political theory, 28; justice as governed by, 122; in legislative deliberations, 3; limits in human affairs, 20, 124; in political psychology, 2; self-assessment and exercise of, 51; self-interest and, 11, 12, 23, 25, 135; societies built on, 5

religion: afterlife and, 29, 79, 80, 87; commerce and, 31–32; culture and, 76, 112; dictates of, 16; in disruption of political order, 62; freedom of, 29–30; in India, 36, 137n2; power of, 18–19, 25; theocracy and, 22; tolerance of, 11, 14; in Turkey, 18–19; zealots, 11, 12, 29. *See also specific religions*

resentment: anger and, 62, 63, 66, 126–27; cognitive component of, 3; fear and, 66; humiliation and, 56, 57, 126; illusions regarding, 22; of injustices, 33, 63.64, 122; mobilization of, 120, 134; politics of, 23, 36, 62–64; power of, 64; repression of speech and, 116. *See also* dark passions

retribution, 98, 122

revenge: collective, 56; desire for, 2, 4, 23, 53, 54, 56, 61, 64, 131; international relations and, 57; motivating power of, 23; territorial irredentism and, 56; Treaty of Versailles and, 125

rhetoric: of Aristotle, 61–62; dark passions mobilized by, 120–27; explanatory, 128–30, 134–35; of FDR, 69, 128–29; of fear, 89–91; Gresham's law and, 3; of Hitler, 126; hope summoned through, 35–36; of identification, 113; Lincoln's Lyceum Address (1838), 101; power of, 132, 134–35; in taming of dark passions, 5, 125, 127–28; Trump's CPAC speech (2023), 121–24; trust created through, 121; weaponization of, 125. *See also* persuasive speech

Rhetoric (Aristotle), 61, 70

Rice, Condoleezza, 21–22

Riefenstahl, Leni, 99

Robin, Corey, 88

Roosevelt, Eleanor, 67

Roosevelt, Franklin D. (FDR): Atlantic Charter and, 69, 88; on confidence, 74, 75, 129–30; constitutional strengths acknowledged by, 67, 75; death of, 144n4; on enemies, 43; on fear, 66–69, 74–76, 130; "Fireside Chat" (1933), 128–31; "Four Freedoms" speech (1941), 69; internment of Japanese Americans and, 90; lack of autocratic ambitions, 91